Be Your Own Guru

Be Your Own Guru

Betty Bethards

The common sense guru!

Inner Light Foundation • Petaluma, California

The Inner Light Foundation is a non-profit, non-denominational organization engaged in teaching, healing, research and publishing. The ILF, formed in 1969, provides a basic meditation technique for self-growth and enlightenment. It also offers self-help methods for interpersonal communication, health and wholeness, mental health and emotional balance. Activities of the ILF include monthly lectures, weekend seminars, spiritual readings, and media appearances. Betty Bethards is the founder and president.

First printing: March 1983
Second printing: March 1985
Third printing: March 1987
Fourth printing: December 1988
Fifth printing: April 1991
Sixth printing: April 1996

ISBN 0-918915-19-8

Cover design and illustration: Jon Goodchild
Printed in the United States of America

This book is lovingly dedicated
to my son Wayne
who crossed over to the other side
on January 12, 1971
And my deep appreciation is
expressed to all who helped make
this book possible, whether they
may be in or out of the body.

CONTENTS

Extraordinary happenings to an ordinary me. The Beginning of Psychic Ability. Approaching the Cross-roads. My Choice to Live. Meeting My Inner Teachers. Asking for Confirmation. A Sign at Last. Changes Again. Finding Self Love. The Heart of the Teachings. Understanding Channeling. Man as an Energy Being. Finding Your Way. Tools and Responsibility.

Ancient Teachers in a Modern World. Understanding Karma and Reincarnation. Beyond Male and Female. What about Free Will? Incarnations Beyond the Earth Plane. The Process of Growth. Learning the Value of Positive Programs. The Conscious and Subconscious Mind. Loving the Self. Programming Your Karma. Letting Go of Karma by Letting Go of Others.

Life and Death, Two Sides of the Same Coin. The Nature of Death. Death and the Sleep State. Earth as School. What Happens at the Time of Cross-Over. After the Homecoming. Religious Beliefs. Society on the Astral Plane. Communication with Others. Understanding Realms Beyond the Earth Plane. Life and Death Cycles on the Other Planes. Helping Ourselves and Others Prepare for Death. Getting a Perspective. Clearing Up Old Guilts. Death as Regeneration.

Preface

Betty Bethards is the common sense guru. She is widely known as a spiritual healer, meditation teacher, psychic and mystic. She has been called a superwoman of the supernatural and one of the top psychic healers in this country.

Her first major publication was *The Sacred Sword* in 1972. The title suggested the two-edged sword of karma that symbolizes individual responsibility: as you sow, you reap. *The Sacred Sword* included her basic teachings on karma and reincarnation, death, psychic phenomena, concentration and meditation, healing, and the significance of this age. No longer available in its original form, it has been revised and expanded in this new book, *Be Your Own Guru*.

Be Your Own Guru carries the original theme of self-responsibility even further. In her folksy, down to earth way Betty again underlines that the only place to look for answers is within, and that sitting on mountain tops and running after gurus is not what this age calls for. It is time, she says, for us to get our personal acts together and to be actively involved in working with our fellows to create a world that works. If we don't, we just won't have a world to worry about much longer.

We are far too gullible, she explains, believing everyone else's ready made answers, buying packages of truth and salvation. We are far too eager to give our personal power away, our free will and responsibility, whenever we have the chance. But no one can save us but ourselves.

Be Your Own Guru offers a common sense message of how to find our way through the maze we've created. It's a message of unsurpassed challenges, tremendous hope, and a barrel full of fun. It begins with Betty's own story, and continues to weave an extraordinary picture of what we're really all about as temporary earth dwellers.

Chapter 1

A Crazy Thing Happened On My Way Through Life

Extraordinary Happenings To An Ordinary Me

One day you may find your life completely turned upside down. It happened to me.

I was twenty-one at the time, had been married for five years, had two children, and was devoted to bridge and bowling. I considered myself an ordinary middleclass wife and mother who enjoyed normal, ordinary things in life.

I was puttering around in my kitchen, washing a few dishes and putting away odds and ends. Suddenly, without any warning, I had an intense cold chill up my spine. I looked around and saw an old friend named Jerry.

Jerry was hovering several feet above the floor. I had attended his funeral one week earlier.

"Go away, you're dead!" I screamed. But he remained, appearing to be in no hurry to leave. He was wearing the same clothes he had been dressed in at the funeral and looked just like he always had to me.

"I must be imagining things," I kept telling myself. After all, being raised a fundamentalist Baptist (later turned Methodist), I believed that when you died you were put in the ground and stayed there until Gabriel blew his horn on the final judgement day. Maybe Jerry had never learned about Gabriel, but here he was manifesting in my kitchen and I didn't want any part of it.

Jerry began communicating with me telepathically. I knew exactly what he was saying to me and what he wanted me to know although he never spoke a word. He told me he wouldn't leave until I agreed to write down specific details concerning the handling of his unfinished business affairs, and send them to his wife.

Reluctantly I did this, throwing in a few questions of my own to determine if this being was really Jerry, and what was going on. I felt rather silly and apologetic as I mailed the business information to his wife, who had just moved to another city. But immediately after I mailed it, Jerry disappeared and never returned.

About a week later I got back a letter: "Betty, I don't know how you did it, but you must have been in touch with Jerry. Your letter answered all my questions about handling final details. Everything checked out. And once again I feel all is well."

I then distinctly remembered events that surrounded his death. The night he died I had felt an overwhelming urge to go to the hospital in the middle of preparing dinner. My husband angrily tried to prevent me from leaving the house, but I got away and arrived just in time to be with his wife after the doctors had pronounced him dead.

I remembered my experience of going to the funeral home. I had never seen a corpse before and was afraid of the prospect. I deliberately arrived early so that I could gather myself together after viewing the body and appear strong and collected for Jerry's wife. I inched my way across the room to the casket and peered in.

Immediately I was filled with a feeling of relief. "That's not Jerry," I thought, "that's an empty shell!" All my fear left me, and I found I was looking around the room trying to find him.

And as I reflected on these experiences, I realized I had been subtly prepared for my friend's abrupt visit.

The Beginning of Psychic Ability

The next ten years were unsettling. I continuously had precognitive dreams about my friends and other various events, and most of the time they came true. I felt an obligation to relate some of these dreams to my closer friends, thinking that if they were aware of the possibility of hardship or danger they could avoid it. But because many of the dreams were about possible unpleasant experiences, my friends began to suggest: "Hey, Betty, do me a favor and don't dream about me tonight."

Remember, of course, that psychic phenomena and parapsychology were not in vogue in the mid 1950's and 60's, and I often wondered if I were going crazy.

During this same ten year period I went through a divorce, remarried and had two more children. I remained an avid bridge player and bowler. I also became quite addicted to working jigsaw puzzles.

Approaching The Crossroads

The family moved often, and we were living in Bellevue, Washington, at the time of my next major spooky experience. I was 32 and was fast approaching a big crossroads in my life.

I returned home one night from a bridge game with a burning sensation in my chest and went right to bed. An hour later I awoke to find myself hovering over the bed about two feet above my body. A voice said to me, "You're going to have pneumonia. Get to a doctor."

Now this was a first. I was so frightened I reached down and pulled myself back in my body again. I had never heard of "out of body" experiences, and had no idea what was happening. Almost in tears, I awakened my husband.

"I was floating above my body," I cried.

"That's okay, honey," he answered sleepily, "It'll be all right in the morning."

With that consoling remark he rolled over and went right back to sleep.

15

But it wasn't all right. The next morning I insisted on going to a doctor. The first one assured me I was fine, to go home and take aspirin. Not satisfied, I went to an internist and asked for a chest x-ray. He looked at me with raised eyebrows, said I didn't have pneumonia, but it was my money if I wanted an x-ray. Sure enough it showed pneumonia beginning in the left lung. Again the prescription was to go home and rest. No antibiotics were given.

For the next two weeks I had temperatures of 103 to 105 degrees, and grew weaker and weaker. I began to wonder whether I was going to make it, and I felt so terrible that I wasn't sure I wanted to. At the end of this period I found myself sitting on the couch in the living room with hardly enough energy to move.

Suddenly I was twenty feet across the room. Everything I considered "Betty" to be--memory, personality, senses--was looking back at that shell on the couch. I thought, "Gee, she's sick. I don't want to go back."

Then a very gentle voice said from behind me, "You don't have to go back, but this is death if you choose to stay."

I had a body which appeared the same, was wearing the same clothes, and was raised about two feet off the floor. I wasn't frightened at all, but felt wonderfully enveloped in peace. I knew then how Jerry had appeared to me ten years earlier. It was as if I could see things clearly, and knew that there was no such thing as death. I realized then that one never dies, but changes vibrations, and goes on living and learning on other levels.

My Choice To Live

I didn't really want to go back. But then I started seeing pictures of my children flash before me. It was a tricky way to get me to make up my mind to return to the earth plane and finish what I was supposed to do. I was fine with seeing each child, knowing they could take care of themselves without me, until I saw my eighteen month old son. I knew he still needed me, and at that point I made my decision. I had to go back.

As soon as I thought this, the voice said to me again, "Unless you take an antibiotic within the next twenty-four hours, you will no longer have a choice of whether you wish to remain on the earth plane."

Immediately I found myself back in the body on the couch. As soon as my husband came home I told him I had to have an antibiotic. We found a doctor, got the medication, and the fever broke almost immediately. But it took over a year for my energy level to return to normal.

It was after this experience that I felt like a confused child. Everything I had ever believed or thought to be true was scratched. My whole belief system was gone. It's one thing to see someone like Jerry manifest before you, but it's a new ball game when you yourself go through a death experience. My idea of reality was completely transformed in one fell swoop, and I didn't know who to turn to.

Meeting My Inner Teachers

My experiences in the next several years continued to be dramatic. I began to communicate telepathically with unseen teachers around me. As my energy grew stronger, old ones would leave and new ones would arrive on the scene. I perceived them as beings of light, and they told me they see us as light beings, not as bodies.

They began to give me teachings I had never heard before and was hesitant to accept. They spoke of reincarnation, karma, and many other ideas that I thought were off the deep end. But I continued to listen because they were so loving and seemed so real, and I would speak as they spoke to me, recording much of the information on tape.

These teachers identified themselves as the White Brotherhood, guardians of mankind. White means light or truth, and has nothing to do with race. They told me that I was to be a channel of love.

Many times I thought I was losing my mind. There was no one to help me understand what might be going on. Maybe I

17

was schizophrenic and making up the whole thing. But how could I be getting all this information?

I went to ministers and doctors for help. Finally, my own minister counseled me: "Betty, as long as what is being told you is good, there seems to be no harm in continuing. Pray for guidance, and ask God how to understand what is happening."

Of course I had been praying for guidance throughout this whole experience, but I was still spending many frustrating hours trying to figure out what was happening. I would have given it up many times if it hadn't been for the constant urging of my husband. He was so intrigued by the whole thing that he would sit with me sometimes four or five hours a night, recording information and offering what assistance he could, as I learned to refine my perception and tune in to these teachers.

My psychic ability and intuition were greatly expanding, and I was able to channel more and more information of a higher caliber from my teachers to those around me. (By channeling I mean my ego or personality steps aside and allows my higher self to tune in to higher frequencies, that is, my teachers or guidance. I can interpret what they say or allow them to speak directly through me using my voice, which then takes on a much deeper quality. It's not the same as mediumship, because I still have control over what is happening and can cut it off at any time.)

What I continued to learn was the importance of control. I went through a few frightening moments, only because I think I needed to experience them to help others avoid similar pitfalls. I learned that one shouldn't fool around with such things as seances, automatic writing, or ouija boards, because you are giving up your sense of control to another power. This can be psychologically dangerous, and in extreme cases lead to schizophrenia. (In fact, I often say that the only difference between a schizophrenic and me is that I have control and can turn frequencies off and on in my consciousness. Those in mental institutions really are seeing and hearing things, but they are on a much lower energy level and have no sense of a personal self with which to identify. They are too wide open, and we must all learn how to protect our energy fields from uninvited intruders, whether in or out of the body.)

I also insisted on having a name for at least one of these beings around me. My teachers explained that names were not important, that the message or teaching was the main point. However, I was given a couple of names for awhile just because guidance felt it would make me more comfortable. But these teachers did not continue with me, either, as I grew to new levels of understanding.

I was taught a simple meditation technique, an ancient Egyptian method, that I was told was the simplest and fastest way to heighten one's energy and expand awareness. It involved sitting for twenty minutes a day, ten minutes in concentration and ten minutes in meditation. I had been practicing it for about a month, getting extremely bored, because I didn't feel I was getting anywhere. If this technique was so great, why was I continuing to stare at the backs of my eyelids instead of getting some great revelation?

Asking For Confirmation

Finally, since I was getting no clarification, I decided to give everything up. I told my husband that I could no longer go on listening to these voices, recording information, working those long night hours trying to make some sense out of everything. I announced loud and clear to my teachers, also, that this was it.

My husband said that if I wanted to quit that was fine, but he planned to go on. He wanted to learn all that he could and continue to explore what was happening. But how could he, I thought. He doesn't see or hear anything. He can't really do it without me. Feeling a little guilty, I decided that once and for all I wanted this thing to be settled. I decided that if I didn't have a sign that this was legitimate, I'd forget it. But I'd give it one more chance.

A Sign At Last

I prayed for four days, asking how to understand the voices, the visions, the teachings. I prayed that I be given a sign if I was to continue, something that would prove to me that this wasn't all just in my head.

At the end of the four day period my husband joined me briefly for a few moments. While we were sitting in silence together, meditating, a sudden rush of energy filled the room. I was levitated off the floor. My first thoughts were: "Oh, God, they're going to drop me on my nose!" But I floated gently down, and that was sign enough for me. I knew I couldn't have imagined it.

Then my guidance began working with me to refine the meditation practice: spine straight, deep breathing, focusing. As I continued in the days ahead I began to feel more confident and centered. I started teaching the technique to others.

I was told that I would be working as both healer and teacher, would lecture widely, would establish a foundation, and would work with psychical researchers, doctors, psychologists, and other professionals. I was also told that I must endeavor to apply the teachings to my own life, and only as I did this would I receive more advanced information.

These things began to happen quite rapidly. In 1969 some associates and I established the Inner Light Foundation, a non-profit, non-denominational organization for the purpose of teaching, research, and publishing. I was establishing hundreds of free meditation and healing groups, and was getting the message out to thousands of people. I began appearing on television and radio programs, and estimated we were reaching several million people every year.

Changes Again

In October of 1970 I had a dream telling me that my oldest son Wayne would be killed in Viet Nam. This was a real blow. Wayne and I shared a special relationship of love and understanding, the quality never being met in my relationship with my husband. Although I prayed that he be spared, I knew that God wanted to take him home. So when I received word of his death in January, 1971, I was somewhat prepared. He had wandered off a main trail, stepped on a land mine, and died instantly.

Wayne appeared to me after he crossed over to tell me that he was all right, and I have seen him on several occasions since then. One of the repercussions of his crossing was I felt a tremendous void in my life. It was about this time I was told that I could not continue to develop my channel unless I had the love energy coming back to me in a one to one relationship. I didn't know what that meant at first, but I began to seriously look at what was going on in my marriage. My husband invested no emotional energy in the relationship. I was cast in the role of mother-counselor most of the time.

When my second oldest son Chris was 7 years old, I had asked my guidance if he would live a long life. They told me that Chris would die young. I learned not to ask for answers that I really did not want to know.

On the evening of April 9, 1983, I had a dream about death. I saw a calendar and then a cute little fat clock with arms and legs running down a path. A man's voice said to me, "Time is running out." I woke up and looked at the time. I wrote on a piece of paper "3:12 a.m., clock running, time is running out."

My door bell rang and I knew immediately that Chris had been killed. Chris's father (my former husband), his wife and my daughter, Pam were at the door. They told me that Chris had just been killed riding his motorcycle on the approach to the Golden Gate Bridge.

Having two of my three sons go home was a very hard life lesson for me. Yet, my death experience had taught me that there truly is no death. We all continue learning and growing in another dimension. My major consolation is that I can now locate my sons easier out-of-the-body than when they were in them: Now, all I have to do is call for them and they're right there!

Finding Self Love

Through all my life experiences, I have been able to help so many others with their lessons in life. It has been especially rewarding for me to be able to help teenagers through those difficult years. It's very important for each of us to develop our self esteem and confidence and pass this on to our children. We need to love and value ourselves, so that we can allow others to come in and love us.

Another challenge I had to face was losing my kidney at age 48. Doctors had incorrectly diagnosed my condition for several months. Finally, my intuition told me it was a kidney problem. By this time I had already lost my right kidney and was on the verge of losing the left one. I immediately went into surgery at the University of California Medical Center in San Francisco. I mentally programmed, "There will be no pain, there will be no complications and there will be fast healing." After the 8 hours of surgery was compleated, I refused all pain killers and didn't even take a Tylenol. My colon didn't even freeze. I was the first person in the history of U.C. to pull this off.

Early on in my development, my guidance had told me that my 5th book would be the most successful one. At age 49, I channeled *The Dream Book,* which has been incredibly successful throughout the country. I am a guest on call-in talk shows weekly across the country and have done numerous television shows on Dreams. The radio phone lines are always filled with callers wanting their dreams interpreted. Dreams are your greatest free tool for receiving help and direction for your daily life from your guidance.

In my mid-thirties I did physical therapy work. I loved being able to help 150 people a year. After that job ended, I told God, "Okay, you show me what you want me to do next."

Several years ago I reached an estimated 10 million people a year through my lectures and media appearances. Now, due to all the national shows, I've lost count! It has been a tremendous reward for me to be as Johnny Appleseed, giving out the seeds for self growth for others.

The last several years have been the first time in my adult life I've been single. Since my children were grown, I had to ask myself, "Who am I? I'm no longer a wife or mother." These have been the greatest years of personal growth and self discovery. I've been exploring my likes and dislikes, who I am and really daring to be me. I've discovered a great strength and peace of mind within me. When people tell me they're afraid of being alone, I let them know that learning to know and love yourself can be the most wonderful and rewarding journey for them. Whether you're single or married, Self Love is our greatest lesson on the earth plane.

The Heart Of The Teachings

But what is this work which I feel so committed to? I often comment that I would do exactly what I am doing with or without pay, because I love it so much.

The heart of the teachings is meditation. They emphasize accepting personal responsibility through getting in touch with the God-self within. My teachers, or guidance, explain that we are accountable for every thought, word, and deed. Our whole purpose here on earth is to learn, to grow in knowledge, wisdom and love. No one can do it for us, because we have free will and must find our own way. Although we would like to go on forever buying easy answers from others, the only way we grow is to awaken our own inner awareness. Each one of us must come to the realization that we are part of the God force. What we seek is within us, and we truly must be our own guru! Of course, there is help and guidance all around us, but we must make the choices in our lives if we want to learn.

A basic part of the message is foreign to my upbringing, which is the idea that you can't learn everything in just one lifetime. So we are given many lifetimes, in many different situations, to practice what we are learning and pass our tests. This is the principle of reincarnation.

Because it takes us a long time to learn many of the lessons, we keep coming back again and again. We continue to return to school here on earth because of the principle of karma: as you sow, you reap. We are responsible for taking charge of our own lives, for helping our neighbors, for accelerating the expansion of consciousness on this planet, and for creating a world of peace. We must listen to and work with others, but we must develop our own intuition so that we may perceive truth for ourselves in each and every situation. My counsel is always, "Take what feels right and chuck the rest." This applies to whatever you hear from any being, whether in or out of the body. Your gut, your intuition, is the teacher or guru within you. This is what you are working to get in touch with and to integrate into your daily life.

I have found that the more I learn, the more I don't know, and the more I want to know. Life becomes very exciting. Whatever I am given I pass on to others, but always with the same advice I was given from my teachers: don't be gullible, try out ideas to see whether they work, and be very pragmatic in your approach. This, I found out, is the beauty of meditation. It really works! It changes your life because it changes you. But you can't take anyone else's word for it. You have to try it out for yourself!

Understanding Channeling

I have been given all these teachings through my channel, or guidance. The teachings are really confirmations of what you yourself learn through your meditation practice.

The most important thing to realize is that everyone has a channel, which is really the higher self. It is a level or frequency of being that we ordinarily are not tuned in to. It is what is called higher consciousness, an energy that permeates our beings and carries with it the perception of purpose, meaning, and the integration of life. It moves within and without time and space, and when we tune in to it we recognize we are unlimited beings.

It is difficult to think of oneself as a composite of frequencies, of energies, when one is accustomed to thinking in terms of self as form. We like to see ourselves as male or female, young or old, and identify with certain definable limits. In order to grow beyond these limits we must learn that we have many forms, that we are energy or spirit incarnating, taking on forms through the eons.

There are many levels of perception, each representing a frequency. The rational or intellectual level of awareness perceives the world through the five senses. Its logic is bound in cause and effect, in the world of time. It keeps us from stepping out in front of a truck, but it is completely useless in understanding higher spiritual realities.

The psychic level, or astral level, is the next highest plane. It opens a door into expanded perception. The psychic moves beyond time and space and operates on higher laws of energy and motion than traditional physics is able to understand. The psychic level deals in information and phenomena. It can know events in both past and future to a high degree of probability. It is in this realm that people often get stuck, being enamored with telepathy, clairvoyance, precognition, psychokinesis, and other manifestations. Basically the psychic level is kid stuff. Often the information one perceives is inaccurate because it is the result of tuning in to several jumbled messages, plus the projection of one's own needs and fears. The accuracy level of predictions by psychics is actually very low because of this.

The psychic level in and of itself has nothing to do with how to live a better life, refine perception, or expand conciousness. Teachers through the ages have warned that it is a trap, because it gives one a false sense of power to know information or events before they manifest in time. Used wisely the psychic sense, as a part of the higher levels of perception, can be an asset to living one's daily life and helping others. Remember the adage: "Seek first the kingdom of heaven, and all this will be added to you." When we have the wisdom of the higher levels, the gifts and abilities of the lesser realms take their proper place.

Much higher than the psychic is the intuitional or mystical level. One who has cultivated these levels of awareness through meditation has a greatly expanded energy field, is in touch with direction and purpose in life, and begins to integrate experiences and lessons from all lives lived. Mystics often have psychic experiences, but they extend far beyond in understanding, awareness, and application of this knowledge. The mystic is at the level of self-responsibility and self-directedness.

I encourage everyone not to get caught up in the games of the psychic, but to continue with meditation, listening to the teacher within, bringing forth the intuitional awareness. My level of awareness is the intuitional/mystical, and having gone through the psychic levels first I am acutely aware of the difference. This is why I encourage everyone to go beyond the light shows and get on with living your life to the fullest.

Channeling, then, is an inner attunement. It means listening to the teacher within, the God within, the guru within, guidance, or whatever you want to call it. We have a free university within us, and we can learn as much as we are able to perceive.

Man As An Energy Being

The following is channeling on *Man as an Energy Being*. It's message is always inspiring to me, and it is particularly appropriate here:

As we begin to tune in to the God force of our own beings, we begin to understand the magnificence of this energy. It is only by going within that we can begin to really get answers to our many questions.

Before this, if you ask questions and receive answers, regardless of the descriptions we use, you do not have the eyes to see and the ears to hear. Many of your questions cannot be answered in words and understood on the earth plane level. But as you go within, you intuitively know the answers.

The knowledge comes to you as a state of mind. It is a state beyond language, beyond the intellect. It is only through tuning in to this state of awareness that you will know, not through our lengthy explanations.

It is difficult to teach the power of the God force to the masses, because people think of themselves as separate from one another and from God. As long as you are seeing things as separate instead of as one unit, one power, you cannot possibly understand the meaning of this force, the love of God within you. You are not separate from one another, nor are you separate from the things on the earth plane which you see.

As you learn to see yourself not as a drop separate from the ocean, but as part of that ocean, you can truly express the totality of your being. You will know how unlimited you are. How can a drop tell you about the power and force of the ocean unless it has united with the ocean and become one with that power?

Your power lies in realizing this Oneness. The force behind the unity is love.

It is very important for individuals to learn to redirect their awareness, to take responsibility for this energy. As people begin to experiment with tuning in this power and get brief glimpses of it, many become frightened of it. Many pull away for fear of misuse, responsibility, or self-discipline. Few are willing to openly explore and experience this energy because they are unwilling to discipline themselves enough to do it. But there is nothing to fear, for this power is that of a loving God, a gift that can awaken you to new dimensions of happiness and aliveness.

To accept this gift requires that you have a purpose, a direction for your life, and that you assume the responsibility for your own growth. Yet for the most part you continue on the merry go round of life, reincarnation after reincarnation, never tapping into that which is freely given within the self.

If you understood this power, this energy, you would never have to struggle to manifest things in this life. You would never have to struggle for peace and harmony, only to attune to that which is within.

Finding Your Way

Another trance I received several years later is actually complementary to the preceding, and sets the tone for this book. It is entitled, *Finding Your Way.*

Many times you may feel confused over what to believe or which path to follow, what is the best direction for your life. You will never know for sure as long as you look without rather than within.

The purpose of each individual's unfoldment is to go within the self, to be one's own guru, to find one's own truth and answers.

There are many good teachers and many good teachings on the earth plane at this time. There are many paths presented, and each one is different. But each will end up on the same mountain top. To know which path is right for you is dependent upon finding the God within. Within that God Head you will know the way for you to go. How you get to the mountain top matters little, but it must be found within your own soul.

If you are always looking for a teacher you will find that your dependency upon such teachers continues to grow. We tend to discourage that because we don't want one individual dependent upon another for his spiritual enlightenment. It is crucial that you be in touch with your own inner light.

You don't have to go to some special place to perceive truth, wear special clothes or follow rigid doctrines and practices. Truth is all around you every day. It can be perceived at any moment, in any place, at any time.

Many people feel they have to reach for a guru in order to have guidance along the path. This is exactly what we tell people to avoid. You do not want to set up a dependency upon another teacher other than the God within yourself. As you grow your ideas change. As you change you will find there are many things a particular teacher feels is true that no longer go along with your belief systems.

This is why it is important to study with many teachers, many people, knowing that you are all fellow seekers along life's path. Take the best tools, the best insights from each teacher, then synthesize them for yourself. What feels right for you is what should be kept. What does not feel right should be discarded.

We discourage people from feeling that they have to have a leader, a way-shower. You are all leaders. You are all teachers. You are all gurus. You are all students. Follow the God within and you will be led divinely so that you may gain knowledge from all people.

You are a child along the path of life who can come forth with even greater wisdom than some well-known guru. How simple it is, that truth lies within. You are willing to go to almost any lengths to know truth: follow a teacher, follow ritual, sacrifice and suffer. You are willing to do almost anything except the one thing that is necessary: acknowledge your own divinity. "Oh no, not me. I'm not really divine, a child of God. I don't really have a guru within that is part of my higher nature, that I must learn to listen to and follow."

It is difficult for you to grasp your true nature. Yet any qualities of wisdom, beauty, truth and love that you project on another are qualities that come from within yourself. You are these things, yet you would give them away, failing to realize the simplicity and beauty of truth.

We are working to get all people to realize that they themselves are the light. When you begin to discover your own light and build it through meditation, people will naturally be drawn to your beacon. This will enable you to teach what you have learned and experienced.

As you become a teacher, your ideas may be right for some, not applicable for others. So always remember that your path should not be forcefully imposed on another. You must always allow other people to follow the path of least resistance for themselves. That which is simplest is going to be the best path for people to follow.

Truth is within every culture, every religion, every background. Truth is not more real because it seems exotic or unusual or because the teacher wears flowing robes or a turban. Truth comes in many forms. It is always nearer to you than hands or feet.

As long as you are attracted to the outer trappings of a religion or the charisma of a guru, you are still not seeing the great truth behind all teachings: Be still, and know the God within.

Tools And Responsibility

What any teacher tries to do is to give others the tools needed for self-development. I can't be, no one can be, all things to all people. When we learn what the tools are for our growth, then it's up to us to use them. We have three free tools, all we really need, which I will discuss further in Chapter 5: dreams, prayer, and meditation.

Today the main tool I provide is meditation. This is a tool for self-awareness and individual responsibility. No one can grow for you, so I help you to help yourself.

Accepting responsibility for our lives, our lessons and learning, is the most thrilling thing with which we can ever come to terms. We can create almost anything we want. There is no one to blame but ourselves for our happiness, unhappiness, success or depression.

But more about this in the next chapter which contains the crux of the message: self-responsibility.

Chapter 2

Karma And Reincarnation: Accepting Individual Responsibility

Ancient Teachings In A Modern World

Karma and reincarnation were hard for me to swallow at first. They were totally foreign to my fundamentalist upbringing. But as they became more and more an integral part of all the teachings I was receiving, I began to see how much sense they made. Before that I could never understand why some people were born blind, some died at a young age, some lived in wealth and others lived in poverty. The human plight just didn't seem fair. Now that I understand we create our own circumstances for very good reasons, and we have many lifetimes to live, it all seems to fit into the picture.

These interwoven concepts have been known in both eastern and western traditions since early times, and once had wide acceptance in the early Christian church. In essence they are easy to understand. Reincarnation suggests that a person is basically spirit or consciousness which takes bodily form, and is born lifetime after lifetime. Literally it means "spirit becoming flesh again and again." Karma refers to the law or principle which governs one's experiences over collective lifetimes and within the individual lifetime. Some people call it the cosmic law of cause and effect, and it simply means that we will harvest exactly what we have planted. It is the principle of individual responsibility: we control our own destiny by our thoughts, words and deeds.

The following information is a composite of trances and other information I have received on the process of reincarnation and karma and what they mean.

Understanding Karma And Reincarnation

Reincarnation is a natural, normal process of the evolution or development of the soul. The process provides the soul with the opportunity to grow and to learn until it is able gradually to raise its level of vibration so that it can enter new dimensions of being.

The soul is the etheric body. The soul is energy. There are layers within the soul because you have many astral bodies, or energy bodies, which you shed the higher you go spiritually. At death you shed the physical body as a coat, and emerge much as a butterfly comes forth from a caterpillar. You do the same thing on each and every level on the other side.

However, if you are to incarnate again, you will keep the added layers or astral exterior of energy until such time as you no longer need to come back to the earth plane. Once you have completed your karmic ties and learned your lessons on the earth plane, having gained balance spiritually, mentally and physically, you then will go to the celestial plane and live in those vibrations.

The whole purpose of the soul's existence here on earth is to free itself from the necessity of endless rebirths. Earth is a school, a place to learn about basic principles of life. Each soul chooses how fast it wishes to progress. Between incarnations one receives many teachings. When the soul returns to earth it brings back the knowledge and training and tries to put it into practical application in the body.

It is very difficult to be loving, kind, gentle and forever forgiving when you find yourself around people who are not of the same caliber. It's easy on the other side because you are only around like-minded beings, and you have much greater awareness. Many choose to incarnate when they don't really have to because it would take the equivalent of 1000 years to do out of the body what you could do on the earth plane in one short sixty to eighty year life period.

There is an ultimate plan that God, or Universal Love, has for all creatures. Ultimately it is that they should find their way back to the infinite love power of the universe. Each individual designs a plan for his growth before each incarnation. One may receive help from teachers on the other side, but the plan is your own choice. So before each soul incarnates on the earth plane, it plans carefully what it hopes to achieve in that lifetime. It decides what strengths or weaknesses it desires to unfold or learn to control. It decides what karma it wishes to work out. The soul is still free once it incarnates to go ahead with the plan or change its mind. Your teachers, of course, are going to be there encouraging you to get on with the program. But we are free to blow an incarnation, and then we will choose to come back and do it all over again.

Why don't we remember all these great resolutions? Memory is largely erased at birth, although the spiritually developed person may see or recall his former lifetimes. Some psychics can see the previous lifetimes of others. Some people come in with such an overriding sense of what they are supposed to do that their career is never a question for them. Child prodigies are individuals with memory and skill which are carried over from other existences.

But everyone can know that he or she has chosen the circumstances of this present life: sex, parents, nationality, race, socio-economic conditions, astrological sign, and so on. The first 28 years of this life you already have knowledge of before you incarnate, and understand exactly what you're getting into. Born out of wedlock, parents divorced, a family of alcoholics, whatever the circumstances, you have chosen them for a reason. If you are adopted, then you have chosen your adopted parents in a very closely coordinated time schedule.

Once you understand that you intentionally selected your present existence, you are able to ask why. There is always a reason. If people could only realize that we have chosen our race, that we have all been many races, there would be no prejudice. People who are prejudiced must return under the same circumstances of those they condemn. We never incarnate into anything but a perfect body unless we choose it. For example, if we are born blind, we are working to develop the higher spiritual senses, deliberately cutting ourselves off from sensory input that can get in our way of listening to the intuitive.

What you perceive of as suffering is actually your opportunity. It is a chance to correct past mistakes and continue toward your ultimate goal. For example, if you blame your parents (or anyone else) for your unhappiness, you can be sure there is karma to be worked out. You will meet them again and again until you can feel compassion and love. In this way every relationship in every incarnation is an opportunity to grow.

Karma follows you from your very first incarnation and continues throughout all succeeding lives. It is something which when you build, you must pay off. Many souls do not have to pay it off in that particular incarnation. They can wait two or three incarnations before they have to face their past ties. You can see karma working in your life today. If you hurt someone, this hurt will come back to you. If you handle situations with love, you are going to be able to conquer not only *your* karma, freeing you, but you are also going to free the other soul. It is in forgiving that you are forgiven. Each soul must be able to understand these basic laws of karma before one will truly be free from oneself: all attachments, desires, and ego identifications. As you create whatever it may be, your heaven or your hell on earth, you will constantly be meeting yourself throughout each and every incarnation.

34

Beyond Male And Female

A spirit or soul has no gender, is neither male nor female. When you come into bodily form, you choose the male or female body depending on what you lack. If, for example, you need to develop the tenderness and love of the mother, you would choose the female body.

Each person has many incarnations both as a man and a woman. You need to learn to see your fellows not as male or female, but as evolving beings. See yourself the same way. You are only temporarily, for this lifetime, a man or a woman. This is not your permanent identity.

Lesbians and homosexuals lack a clear understanding of the sex role they have chosen. They are in a transitional incarnation. A homosexual may have been a woman in his last incarnation, and still feels like a woman. If he goes to all the trouble of getting a sex change operation, he may or may not find himself in a better psychological condition. He had chosen the male body for a good reason, to help him learn certain lessons, to develop certain strengths. After the operation the lessons remain the same. One should not feel guilty over a sexual preference, but should always continue to explore what the lessons are in this lifetime: Why did I choose this body? Why did I choose these circumstances?*

What About Free Will?

The will is the entity's directional force. It is the power of will which enables us to direct our lives, to make choices. The will represents an individual's strength. It is the developing ability to select wisely our pathway of growth, to carry out the intent of our life plan. The will goes with one from incarnation to incarnation. It is the developing awareness of purpose, the steering mechanism that keeps us pointing forward. Will is the determination to persevere in the process of working out one's karma through numerous rebirths.

---

*These topics are more fully explored in *Sex and Psychic Energy*.

There are many arguments over whether man really has free will. From the reincarnation standpoint, we do to a large degree. We choose our pace, how rapidly or slowly we will progress. We choose our circumstances, how and when and where we will work out our karma.

We choose our actions, specific deeds, attitudes, and responses in the various relationships of life. We are always free to decide how we will respond to the situation in which we find ourselves, and that situation is itself a result of our freely chosen deeds.

Practically, there are limitations on the will rooted in the nature of physical reality. Once you choose a framework or the particular circumstances for a lifetime, you are restricted to operating within that framework. For example, if you choose to be born with a six foot brown skinned male body, you cannot suddenly decide you wish to be a petite five foot yellow skinned female. But within our framework we have all the freedom we need, and far more than we can use, for progressing in our life tasks of growth.

Incarnations Beyond The Earth Plane

There are life vibrations on all the planets in our solar system, and in the solar systems throughout the universe. We have dwelled on many of the planets in other forms, learning other lessons there. Where we choose to manifest, whether on earth, as a physical body, or on another planet as a light body, is the result of what we wish to learn and what our own vibrational rate happens to be. We may choose to learn and grow in other spheres when we are ready.

Whether we are on the earth or other planes we are responsible for our thoughts and deeds, and must pay off our karma on the plane where it is collected.

The Process Of Growth

The following is a channeling on karma and reincarnation that provides a thumbnail sketch of the purpose of the process:

Chapter 3

Transitions: Understanding Death

Life And Death, Two Sides Of The Same Coin

We all have died many times. The problem for most of us, however, is that we just don't remember. This was certainly true for me until I had my first death experience and was given the choice of whether I wished to return to the earth vibration or stay on the other side.

It was my first death experience that completely ended all my old beliefs about the nature of reality, what life is really all about, and why we are here in the first place. For many, such an experience is very frightening, or sobering I should say, because you begin to realize that there is absolutely no escaping from yourself! Life is eternal, and we go on and on, meeting ourselves, our fears, over and over, until we finally decide to love ourselves and get on with the program.

If we are ever to come to terms with the meaning of our lives here on earth, we must learn to understand death.

It is only then that we can see with a total perspective, fitting all the pieces of the puzzle together.

Otherwise, nothing makes much sense. If we identify ourselves with our physical forms, our brains and bodies, all the striving and learning we undergo in a given lifetime must seem rather futile.

Of course, after you have been meditating for awhile you lose all fear of death, because you begin to transcend dimensions in your meditation. You realize that you exist on many realms simultaneously, and only the physical body is shed when you finally check out of the earth hotel.

Before death became a popular topic I was receiving a great deal of channeling on the nature of death: what happens when we die, how to understand the other side, how to help others who are facing death. I was told how to integrate an awareness of death into our daily lives so that we are able to live fully, moment by moment. This chapter provides a composite of information from my channel which I have received during the last several decades.

The Nature Of Death

Life is eternal. There is no *death*. If people correctly understood death, they would no longer have any fear of the unknown. Death is but an inevitable transition that each soul makes when it leaves the physical body. It is a freer state which does not limit the soul to time and place.

Death is a change in the rate of vibration. The energy force or soul which is the real you sheds the lower vibration of the physical body at death. The body returns to dust, because the etheric or energy body no longer resides within the physical vehicle. In the state of so-called death, the energy, your spirit, leaves the physical body and does not return. Your personality, memory, everything you consider to be you will leave with this energy because you are energy.

What we think of as *life* and *death* are merely transitions, changes, in the rate of vibration in a continual process of growth and unfoldment. The Life energy, God, underlies all experiences of life and death and is the Changeless. We will never be free from the cycles of death and rebirth until we come to know this Energy behind all appearances, all cycles, all stages of growth. When we know the One, the ground of our true being, we begin to identify with our eternal nature, rather than the stages we are going through at any particular moment in any particular lifetime. To know the Self is to know all things.

Death may be thought of as a graduation. There are no accidental deaths. When one leaves the earth plane it means the soul has done all it wanted to do or was supposed to do, and that there is no longer any need to remain on the physical plane during that specific incarnation.

It is, in fact, more difficult for one to be born than to die. When the soul is born into the world it must lower its rate of vibration to take on the physical form. It must give up certain levels of expanded awareness in order to learn and grow through the lessons of the earth plane. At death one may once again return to a higher and finer vibration.

—— STOPPED HERE 5/8/99

Death And The Sleep State

As you go to sleep at night, and your consciousness leaves the physical body, you are experiencing the same thing as death. See yourself in the dream state. What do you look like there? You are able to take on many forms and faces, to create adventures for yourself. The body that is you in the dream state is your etheric body, the same you will have at death.

The only difference between the death state and dream state is that the silver cord, which is an energy link much like an umbilical cord connecting the soul with the body, is severed in death. This cord allows the being to travel in the various realms and planes beyond the physical at night to receive higher teachings. In the state of so-called death, the entity severs itself from the physical body in much the same way one was severed from the mother's womb. The energy link, the silver cord, disconnects as the entity leaves the body. All knowledge gained while in the physical form is taken with you. When you leave you could care less about the physical vehicle, because you see it as a hindrance, a prison.

Death is nothing more than birth into a new form. Souls must continue to move to planes and levels of awareness where they can best function and accomplish the greatest amount of growth.

Earth As School

When the soul has chosen to incarnate into physical matter on the earth plane, it enters the fetus in the womb of the mother. When it is time for the child to be born, the soul is then fully released into the physical matter of the new being, and must struggle on its own as an individual entity.

The being is met with earthly temptations, primarily those concerning whether one will be selfish or loving toward others. These experiences help one attain the knowledge needed in order to move toward one's ultimate spiritual destiny.

The earth plane is the most difficult school that an entity goes through. Many times we don't *pass*, but we don't fail either. We just remain on a particular level without progressing. In time we begin to progress at our rate of speed. And, of course, the more we can change inwardly, the more we can comprehend. The more clarity and understanding we have and the more love we are able to bring into our aura, the faster our tests can come.

You can be allowed three or more grades, or three or more lifetimes, in just one incarnation if your soul is truly advancing and learning. This is your soul's choice. If you begin to watch how you handle things, how you are responding to others around you, and learn the lessons from your immediate experiences, you will be given even more tests so that you can continue to accelerate your growth.

What Happens At The Time Of Cross-Over

When the soul has been exposed to the opportunities it chose for a particular lifetime, it is allowed a release from the physical body. The soul knows when the time for release has come.

It is helpful to remember that we have died before, and often we are able to remember past death experiences. They may surface as fears about water, cave-ins, disease, fire, or however we may have died, until we are able to move beyond the fear level in our meditation and realize why we choose particular methods to cross-over.

Death is not the same for everyone. It depends upon how you have prepared yourself during that incarnation, how old a soul you are, how evolved your awareness, and what lessons you chose to learn through the death experience. You may have chosen to learn courage and to build strength through a physical death with suffering. People who die slow deaths from such things as cancer or strokes are often givers who have never learned how to receive. Their souls may choose a slow death in order to allow others to give to them. But you can learn your lesson and move beyond the need for pain and suffering in dying. You may, in fact, have chosen a fast and easy death. Either way it is not a punishment, but a process of growth for both you and those around you. It allows you and others to work through difficult situations with kindness and compassion.

When you approach the time of death, often you're able to see relatives who have crossed over standing around you. The etheric body slips easily in and out of the physical, and many times a person near death talks to beings who are invisible to others. Doctors for the most part think you are hallucinating, but you're not. Whether death comes rapidly or slowly, your loved ones know ahead of time when you are coming, and are there, prepared and waiting, happy that you have been released.

First, you may experience your whole life flashing in front of you much as a drowning man reports this experience. Next, you will go through what appears to be a dark tunnel or dark tube which has a very bright light at the end. Most entites are just drawn to the light without anyone saying, "Go to the light." It's a past soul memory of having left the body many times, and knowing what to do.

As you go through this dimension, you will see souls lined up on both sides around you. Many look pitiful and cry out. You will see them as real people. But they are there because they have chosen to be, and at this point you cannot help them. You must remember to move ahead, following your point of light, and not be afraid.

This light is from higher astral levels, and you follow it to the one you have earned. However you have lived your life on the earth side determines how high you can go into the light on the other side.

There is nothing to fear. There is no way you can be harmed. Fears are within, and this is why you must work to release yourself from fears on the earth plane, because you will carry these same fears over to the next dimension.

But not all are immediately propelled into the light area. Some people will be blocked into a gray, hazy state, much like you would feel a fog all around you. You don't have clarity; there's neither the darkness nor the light. This occurs when there has been much negativity during an incarnation, or a suicide when one must spend some time contemplating what has happened. This grayness is similar to a purgatory or limbo state. It is a holding place where souls who are confused, who do not want to let go of their earthly attachments, or who choose not to grow will remain until such time as they allow themselves to be released to flow once more into the light.

Purgatory is a place of your own making. We see souls who are punishing themselves here on the earth plane. This continues after death just the same as it would if they were still in the physical body. Many people must suffer in order to feel worthy. When they finally learn this is a negative number they are running, they can move on.

Some people may want to hang around their old surroundings on earth rather than go on to discover for themselves the beauty and wisdom which is offered to them on the other side. This may take a long time, but they are coaxed along slowly. Nothing is forced on a soul, neither attitudes nor understandings. This is why we are always counseled here on earth never to force our beliefs on another person until he is ready to hear them. The free choice of every individual should be acknowledged.

Normally when you die you are shown loved ones first so

that you may understand what has happened. You are given glimpses of things you expected to see in order to bring you comfort. You may briefly see a teacher you worshipped in your lifetime: Jesus, Buddha, or another guru, according to your expectations. After the first seventy-two hours, however, you are gently brought out of many of your illusions and shown that you have not landed in an ultimate paradise with gold paved streets. Of course you could choose to create these for yourself on this plane, but once you truly understand you would most likely choose to be around that with which you felt most comfortable.

If you don't believe in God or an afterlife, you will probably be kept in a sleep state for the first two to three day period. You will wake up in a beautiful meadow or some other calm and peaceful place where you can reconcile the transition from the death state to continuous life. You are given teachings in the hope that you do not refuse to believe that you are dead.

There is always good at the time of your cross-over. Even people who have lived lives of selfishness will know and understand the rejoicing. Whatever you have sown you are going to reap in terms of structuring your experiences and lessons which continue on the other side. But the first few days of cross-over (as you know time on the earth plane) you are allowed to be with your teachers and those who have loved you in the past.

On the other side you see things with a clearer, more objective nature, but you are not given total knowledge because you would not understand it or be ready to use it, any more than while you are here on earth. We are given knowledge only as we are ready to receive it, whether we are in or out of the body.

After The Homecoming

After the first several days of welcome and rejoicing, the soul meets with what may be called a loving board of directors. It is composed of teachers and other higher beings who have walked with you. These beings help you review your past life, to begin to look at what was learned and not learned, and what you wish to work on or do from this point. No one judges you, and this is important to keep in mind. You are the one that judges yourself and decides what is best for continued growth.

The record of your life is very private. Only those who have walked with you as teachers are allowed to see what is called your akashic record. If during your lifetime you ask that a psychic tune into this record, he or she will only be given a minimal amount of information from it which is particularly relevant to your immediate problems or concerns.

As you are ready, and as you choose, you will be shown your past lives. If you do not believe in reincarnation it may take a long time before you are able to deal with this. Eventually you must learn to understand yourself in a continuity of growth over many lifetimes. You must recognize all the strengths you have built and all the karmic ties you have created which must be dissolved.

By the time you are given the privilege of reviewing all past lives and integrating the knowledge learned, you will have reached a state of total objectivity. You will feel no remorse or condemnation, but will see it as merely a review of why situations occurred and had to be worked through.

You will be given teaching, training, and anything you need to help you prepare yourself for your next incarnation. But this is not given immediately. You can choose your own pace and need not be hurried through the planes in the next dimensions. It may take centuries for your soul to know what is best for your development once you return again to a physical body. It may take a great deal of reflection before you determine a purpose and direction for your next sojourn on earth.

Also, as part of your training, you are allowed to watch people on the earth plane to see how they handle situations when they reincarnate. Very few people in a physical body realize that their behavior is a teaching ground for those who are out of the body.

Religious Beliefs

Your religious beliefs have little to do with what you experience in the transition from one realm to another, except that you would be allowed to see briefly the teacher or guru that you followed. What counts is what comes from the heart, not what one professes to believe. It means nothing whether or not one was baptized, for example, or whether one has various other rites administered. How ridiculous to rely on meaningless words!

The true meaning of baptism is an initiation of the spirit, an opening awareness to the God consciousness. People receive this inner baptism when they are spiritually prepared.

You will not suddenly be sitting at the feet of a man with a long white beard called God. God is within, whether you are in or out of the body. Your awareness of the God force will not be greater on the other side. If you insist upon searching for God, you will do this for awhile until you get the idea that you are following an illusion. My channel has said that we must go through at least four more planes beyond the astral before we could even begin to understand the energy of the God force.

Angels? Yes, such beings are there. They are entites who have gone through their own evolutionary process on a much higher level than the people of the earth plane. Each one of us is assigned one of these beings, as I mentioned earlier, who walks with us during life as our guardian angel. This being merely watches and records how we handle situations, arranging for us to meet those we have karmic ties with. The guardian angel loves you but remains aloof and very patient.

What about the reality of a place called hell? There is such a level, a lower plane than the earth. It is a lonely place where one is not allowed to be in communication with anything other than one's own negativity, and those thought forms are very ugly and powerful.

Souls do not enter this level unless they need to experience it for their growth. Many people who commit suicide will have to go through this hell of their own making in order to become aware that this is not what they are striving for. The soul must learn that it does not have the right to take its own life, that it cannot kill, it cannot hurt other people.

Many people at one time or another have experienced this plane. Children who have nightmares are going into this realm. Alcoholics going through the DTs, people on drugs, may also see it. It is a plane of total darkness where we must confront the fears we have built within our own minds. Understand that fears have no reality unless we choose to give them reality. As soon as we are able to meet them directly, to face them, they dissipate. This lower level is not for one's punishment, but rather to provide the opportunity to confront and move beyond the negativity created by oneself.

The hell fire mentioned in many traditions is symbolic of the kundalini energy (Holy Spirit, God energy, or Creative energy) that dwells within the seven energy centers or chakras within man. Fire is symbolic of the cleansing and purification of the soul.

The balance between positive and negative tendencies within man represent the struggle between the higher and lower self, or what some call God and the Devil. It is this tension between the two that causes growth and learning, until finally the negativity or the destructive elements are completely overcome.

Society On The Astral Plane

Through questions and answers I have received information about what it is actually like to be on the other side. First, my channel has pointed out that the laws are much more protective. We need no longer be exposed to both good and evil, for we have already experienced that. We see the bad only if we choose to. Those who are living in harmony will not be imposed upon by the ignorant, but can visit the lower planes to help another if they choose to do so.

For example, if you loved someone who is on a lower vibration than you are, you may be allowed periodic visitations. This may help the entity greatly by educating him in the need for love and growth. However, the entity will need to incarnate again on the earth plane to test out these new lessons, because it is the earth experience that determines your stage of evolution.

Once you cross over you may choose to do whatever you wish. You may lie in the sun all day, go fishing, whatever interests you. Many people realize they had not taken the time to develop their creative aspects while on the earth plane, due to many karmic ties which had to be worked out. They, then, will take the time to do some of these creative things.

People who are writers will continue to write, those who love music will continue to be involved in music, and so on. There are enormous libraries, universities, all types of creative outlets and sources of information. The soul can learn anything it chooses to learn. All one has to have is the desire to learn and the belief that you can accomplish this. Life does not stop when you cross over: it begins.

Whatever you can imagine, you can create, because all is built through the imagination. Lovely homes, beautiful gardens, snow-capped peaks, every kind of environment you would want is available to you. The color and sound are far more beautiful on the astral than on the earth plane because they are higher and purer frequencies. On the earth plane you create through your imagination, but it takes awhile to manifest because you are living within time and space. On the other side what you imagine manifests instantly. It is important to work on increasing your creative side while on earth, because what you are imagining you are creating not only on the earth plane but in the realms beyond.

You may manifest whatever is pleasing to you, whatever you are comfortable with. You may create country cottages, banquets, jewels, whatever you desire. There is no condemnation for wanting those things or images. Eventually, you will elevate your consciousness above the astral realm and these images will seem less important. You will find that you lose much of your desire for them. But as long as they bring you pleasure and you enjoy them you are welcome to them.

There are unions of souls on the other side, and marriage as such is optional. If couples prefer to remain together they may do so, as long as their interests and growth are taking them in the same direction. If they choose to go in different directions there are no hurt feelings. There is no possessiveness or demands. You are free to go your own way, in your own time, at your own choosing.

Married couples may be reunited after death, and may choose to stay together if they want to, provided they are on the same level of vibration. This is free will. If you have been married three or four times, you will find that you will want to be with the one whom you truly love. It could even be someone from another incarnation. You will be with those you love, and there is a total merger which is a much higher experience and a deeper love bond than anything which you can know on the earth plane.

This total merger is like stepping inside of one another's auras, a total blending of energies. It's a way of expressing love and sharing. What you know on earth as a sexual relationship takes the form of a higher merger of souls. There is no need for sexual organs on the other side unless you choose to have them. For this merger of energies is far superior to the physical mechanics of the sexual experience. This merger is not limited to husbands and wives, but may be experienced by any two souls who are loving and caring.

Communication With Others

Just as we learn to communicate through telepathy here on the earth plane with other people as we develop our awareness, so we communicate on the other side. There is a common telepathic communication among all souls. All languages are instantly translated into what the individuals speak and understand. There is no language barrier, for you understand everything that is related to you. Your thoughts and the thoughts of others consequently are heard on every realm and every level. It takes only a few days to learn the ease in communicating telepathically when you first cross over. This leads to a great deal of growth on the part of the soul, for one is truly learning communication after death. You will know everyone's thoughts, views, and feelings like you were never allowed to know in the physical vehicle.

You can tune into anyone around you like dialing a radio station. But most souls, after the first few days of listening to the thoughts of others, get bored and go on to other things. It would be like you had 200 people in one room, and you could hear their thoughts, their ups and downs, night and day. You would soon grow weary of listening to their disharmonies.

People radiate a light which shows where they are coming from, and others know simply by looking at the aura. Nothing is hidden. Everyone is in this same level of communication. It is not a threatening, but an enlightening experience.

Understanding Realms Beyond The Earth Plane

My channel has explained that there are seven planes, and within each are seven more levels. People may basically look alike, operating in similar physical vehicles, but each person is manifesting at a different rate of vibration depending upon one's evolution. This is why some people are more spiritually advanced and others more material. People of a similar evolution tend to mingle here on the earth plane.

Each plane is a vibratory rate. We may ask, where are these planes. But we have to remember that we cannot grasp the idea of higher dimensions by thinking in terms of time and space as we know it.

The planes are right where we are now, inherent within the soul. All higher planes are within and around you, intermingled with the earth plane. You experience the level to which you have learned to attune your consciousness. When you have learned the lessons of a particular vibration, such as learning the lessons of the earth vibration, you may move on to a finer vibration of experience.

61

When you die you don't go anywhere, no homes in the sky. You are instantly in the fourth dimenson. Remember that heaven is not a place. It is a state of being, an attunement. It is dependent upon self, for self makes its own heaven or hell.

Beings who have crossed over are living at a different rate of vibration right where we are now. You could have a church sitting on top of your house and you wouldn't know it. A train could run through your living room and you wouldn't see it. Only as you raise your vibrations are you going to be able to see life around you as it exists in other realms. And this happens through raising the energy level of the etheric body through meditation.

My channel has named only the next two planes: the one immediately beyond the earth is the astral, and the next highest is the celestial. A soul goes to the celestial only after it has gained that perfect balance within itself and has completed all earthly karma. And from that level no one has to incarnate again.

But, if you choose, you can return for a life of service. Then you go back, putting on your astral coat and physical body, to work with mankind. Once you enter the earthly realms, however, you are open for karma. If you create any it must be worked out immediately as you will have no other life in which to do it.

The majority of people presently on the earth plane will reincarnate although there are some who can complete their earthly karma in the present incarnation. It is through self-discipline, prayer, meditation and patience. We must align ourselves to higher vibrations. We are always free to choose whether to control the emotions or let the emotions control us. And this is the key: emotional control, plus total balance physically, mentally and spiritually.

Life And Death Cycles On The Other Planes

Once you have completed going through the death cycles of the earth plane, you never again go through one. As you advance to the higher planes you experience rather an initiation which takes place to shed the outer layer (as when you shed the physical body). The heavier matter which makes up your coat for one level is shed for a lighter coat when you move to the next. You shed your old beliefs and lessons and attune to your new body, a little like a snake shedding its skin. (People who are meditating are constantly lightening their bodies in order to receive higher and higher teachings. You cannot reach knowledge which is beyond your rate of vibration without raising your consciousness to that point.)

These planes extend throughout the universes. There are other universes which we do not know of intermingled with ours at a different rate of vibration. Millions of planets throughout the cosmos have life and death cycles equivalent to our earth plane life cycles. There are a few universes which have planets identical to earth. But within our own universe, there is no other planet with the same rate of vibration with people who look as we do. The inhabitants are a different frequency, a different rate of energy. Some of these beings have been sighted, and are often described as having a blue light emanating from them. This is because they are lighter than physical matter and more light shines through.

There are special vibrations associated with each planet, and each level within each planet. Our choice of realms and places is dependent, again, upon our level of perception and what we are learning. We go back to various planets in between earth incarnations to study.

Helping Ourselves And Others Prepare For Death

People tend to fear what they do not understand, and certainly the process of death falls into this category. Very few people until recently ever talked much about dying and how one might feel as he or she made the transition.

The prophets of old and all truly great religious teachers tried to help people realize that death does not exist, that it is merely a transition or rebirth. They tried to explain symbolically that man dies only once within the self, and that this death is the death of the lower self going into God consciousness. The death or relinquishing of a limited consciousness is not understood, for the most part, and people fear the natural transition from one state to another. It means nothing more than continuing growth.

Many of the original translations of the various world scriptures which were very clear on the meaning of continuing life have been lost. Jesus, Buddha, and other great sages talked of the continuation of life, but many of these teachings were misunderstood. It is because this truth has been hidden from most of us that we are not free from the fear of the unknown.

Although popular level religions have talked about heavens and wonderful rewards in the afterlife, the sadness and somber ceremonies surrounding funerals created fear, guilt, and misunderstanding in people's minds. People often have horrible ideas about death which they suppress, never accepting the fact that one day they, too, must die.

There are many, of course, who do not fear death. These people have proven to themselves through out of body experiences, meditation, or other processes of heightened awareness that death does not exist in the way they have been taught. Many are able to see those who have crossed over, have had death experiences themselves, or have had loved ones appear to them in dreams and tell them about life on the other side.

Most of our responses toward death are learned. Children have little sense of death because they are so closely attuned to the intuitive side of their nature. They know only life, and cannot conceive of themselves as not existing. Parents, for the most part, do not think children can understand death and so they do not answer their questions honestly, or cannot because they themselves don't know.

Recently I counseled with a mother and her five year old daughter about the death of the husband. The child asked me many questions, such as, "Why did God take my Daddy away?" "Is God punishing us by taking Daddy?" All these feelings are there and should be dealt with openly. I told her that her Daddy was still with her, and that it had just been his time to go home. He had finished what he was supposed to do on earth for this life.

She said, "I know he's all right because I talk to him." Children, much more so than adults, can often see and communicate with those who have crossed over. They should be encouraged in their understanding of continuous life from their very first experience with a physical death, whether it may be an animal, friend, or family member.

As we get older the fear of death is often really a fear of life. We are too afraid to live our daily lives, and so we have this haunting feeling that there is something we're supposed to be doing, getting on with the program, and we aren't doing it. When one feels that life has been lived to the fullest there is no remorse at the time of physical death.

A very sad situation developing today is that of teenage suicides. This represents a total misunderstanding of the whole life process. Young people who have everything to live for are too baffled by the pressures around them, and those who might offer a listening ear often do not think that their problems are important. It is helpful for us to remember that questions we ask and problems we deal with at every age are important, and that each step along the way lays the foundation for either future confidence or confusion.

But how are we to offer help to our fellows if we have not been honest and open with ourselves, endeavoring to look at and move beyond our own fears and limited understanding? This is a time when we must be involved with our own self-awareness so that we may reach out and help those around us. The world today needs a lot of help! Overcoming the fear of death changes our whole perspective on life. Everything we do and think and feel takes on new meaning. When we realize that we are not limited by the physical, we begin to get the idea that we are really master of our own destinies and we more fully align ourselves with the eternal nature of our beings.

Getting A Perspective

There are several things to remember that are very important in getting a wider perspective on death: the departed entity's feelings toward the funeral, loved ones and the grieving process; how we can overcome the energy loss when a loved one dies; how we can rid the self of hurts or guilts which weren't resolved before another crossed over.

First, every one of us is allowed to attend our own funeral. If you ever wondered what cousin John really thought of you, you will have your opportunity to find out. You get to see and hear the thoughts of all present, whether they really thought you were a great person or a jerk. Also, you will feel absolutely no identification with the physical body, and certainly not with a strange graveyard you may happen to be stuck in. Yet every time someone in your family journeys out to put flowers on your grave you will be pulled back to be there.

When my son's body was in the mortuary after being returned from Viet Nam, I was on my way to visit him for the second time. As I got in the car, I heard a sigh over my shoulder: "Oh, mom, do we have to go through that again?" It was then I realized if I had to go he had to go, and he was much more comfortable at home. Needless to say, that was the last time I went.

It is actually better for the deceased to be cremated, because it has a more complete psychologically releasing effect both on those who remain on the earth plane and on the entity.

My channel explained, *The soul usually will prefer a cremation to a burial. Burial causes people to go out to the cemetery and grieve. With cremation and scattering of ashes it is easier for the soul who has entered the so-called death state. It then does not have to keep going to the graveyard which it has to do if people are grieving there. Every time people go to view the grave or to put flowers on it, the soul must go, and the soul really can't relate to that body in the ground. The soul has used it, the body has fulfilled its purpose,*

66

but now it has no meaning whatsoever. The soul sees no reason to set up a tribute to that body which has nothing to do with the real being anyway.

By choice entities may return to be with loved ones and relatives on earth in times of crises or on special occasions, such as holidays and celebrations. Also, they may appear to you and communicate with you in your dream state, or you may sense their presence during a meditation period. This simply reinforces that they haven't really gone anywhere, and that we are all a part of the same universal energy.

It is normal to grieve over the loss of a loved one, but we should remember that the pain is our sense of loss and has nothing to do with the state of the entity who has crossed over. The entity is experiencing a joyous reunion, and we are feeling sorrow at losing physical contact with the entity.

If we can understand that there is a perfect time and place for each of us to leave the earth plane, and that the being who has gone has completed his or her tasks for the lifetime, then our period of crying should be greatly lessened. Your thoughts of grief and sadness, if continued, will pull the entity back to the earth vibration when it really has much better things to be doing. We should really focus on sending love energy and support, a sense of excitement and well-being, to the one who has departed. This energy of love and joy will help propel the soul into its new experience in the higher realms.

Also, when an infant dies it is primarily a lesson for those around the infant. It always means that the child is a very old soul, bringing the parents a special lesson about the love of God. These children are special gifts to their parents, although this lesson is often missed by the distraught mother and father. When the very young die it means they have finished their work on the earth and should not be forced to stay around after their lessons are learned. We can leave as soon as we have learned what we set for ourselves.

We should consciously tell our loved ones that we are releasing them, sending them on with Godspeed. Often a person will hang on to the physical body, postponing the actual time of physical death, because someone in the family refuses to mentally release the person. We must realize that death is a continuing process of growth and that we should not stand in the way of another's development. We should always put the person in God's hands, releasing the soul mentally to God's perfect plan.

When a member of a couple dies, especially if they are old, often the other partner will follow within a year. This happens because the polarity of energy between them has been broken, and one member is taking that energy link which fed the other. If a couple has grown old together without establishing close outside friendships, activities, or other things from which they draw energy, then one will usually die shortly after the other. If they have been meditating over a period of years then they would have established their energy link with the love force, and would easily sustain themselves independently.

Remember that even a healthy person may suffer when he loses the loved one he was depending upon for energy. It is important to stay active, be around positive people, get involved in projects that help continue your growth. Working with children is especially helpful, because you not only are able to help them, but are revitalized by their energy fields. Sometimes when people grow old there may be five to ten years when they have a choice of whether to continue on or leave. One can cause the body to die sooner with depression and discontent. We have an obligation to live, and should make the most of our time in the body. But even if you are working to rebuild your energy, remember that it may take about a year to return to your normal energy level after a close loved one crosses over.

Clearing Up Old Guilts And Grudges

To be completely free from karmic attachment you must release yourself and others. Often when a person crosses over we feel there is something left unsaid or undone. We feel guilty, hurt, angry, or still involved in a negative way with the entity. At this point you should practice forgiving, releasing and moving on. You can always clear karma with another whether in or out of the body, by picturing the person in your mind and talking together. Imagine that you are thanking one another for all you learned together. Remind each other that all the experiences you shared were jointly created to promote growth and insight. Then send one another love and affirm that each releases himself and the other to love, learning and continuous growth. Remember if you harbor negative feelings toward yourself or others, whether in or out of the body, you will limit your awareness and retard your growth.

Death As Regeneration

Death as a process of regeneration is an ancient theme. Traditions of old taught one how to die, the stages one goes through, and how to maintain awareness and experience the process fully. It is only because we have separated ourselves from an awareness of our true spiritual nature that the idea of death sounds grim and foreboding.

If we meditate daily, by the time we are ready to shed our physical bodies the process of changing vibrations and entering expanded levels of consciousness will be old hat. It will be something we can look forward to after a job well done on the earth. We can participate fully in the experience. It is too beautiful an experience to miss through fear or ignorance!

Sometimes people are given a close brush with death in order to reroute them into a more positive state, making them more aware of the special role they have chosen to fulfill in this incarnation. Those who have death experiences, who medically die and then return to their bodies, have been given this experience in order to bring about a drastic change in their way of thinking. In many cases their life beforehand was being wasted, and afterwards they work to help others in a life of service.

69

To see death in its beauty is also to realize the beauty of life on earth. It is a great privilege to be allowed to incarnate because we have the opportunity to learn so much so quickly. No state of awareness is permanent, and we are constantly changing the way we choose to express cosmic energy, which is the ground of our beings. We move from one form to another, one manifestation to another. Eventually we merge our consciousness with the formless, the God energy, which manifests through all life expressions, all forms.

Chapter 4

Psychic Phenomena: Expanding Our Realities

Doorways To Expanded Realms

We get glimpses of other realities, those not limited to the five senses and the rational mind, through dreams, meditation, prayer, and psychic phenomena, to name but a few ways. Psychic phenomena, when they occur in our lives spontaneously, are usually the most jolting. This is because we cannot explain them, and they seem to come from out of the blue.

This chapter presents information on exploring the psychic realm. Serious research in this area has been slow in getting off the ground, and did not really get started in this country until after the American Association for the Advancement of Science officially recognized the emerging science of parapsychology.

The decade of the seventies saw a lot of improvement in both lay and scientific interest. Universities began to add courses in parapsychology, sponsor conferences, and some even offered degrees in the field. More scientists conducted research in the area, more psychics became public figures, and many popular level programs and books teaching how to enhance psychic awareness were on the market.

I, too, worked with researchers in the early seventies to further explore my psychic ability. The abilities I have include clairvoyance, clairaudience, clairsentience, precognition and retrocognition. One of the main problems in psychic research is repeatability, because a person cannot maintain a high level of psychic accuracy all the time. Many experiments have been done to improve accuracy. For me, the more I meditate the higher my energy level, the clearer my attunement to people. I can tell someone what I do when I give a person a reading, but I can't scientifically explain what process is going on.

When I tune in to people, for example, I lock into their energy field through concentration. I receive feelings and impressions about the person, sometimes I hear things psychically, occasionally I catch a vision or two. I feel things more than I see and hear them. But I perceive the other person's guidance, the teachers around him or her, and can answer various questions that one asks me about life, purpose and direction.

Everyone Is Psychic

The exciting part about this is that everyone is psychic, and each person can learn how to enhance this ability and use it to be more productive in one's life. Psychic experiences in and of themselves are actually not from a high level of perception, but come mostly from the astral realm. Being psychic or knowing things about yourself and others through psychic means does not necessarily make you a better person or accelerate your personal growth. This is why teachers of many spiritual traditions warn their students about getting trapped in the psychic realm. The phenomena can be fascinating, but it is only kindergarten stuff, and we need to move to the mystical, or intuitive level, which lies beyond.

The most promising thing about a psychic experience, perhaps, is that it shows you there are other things operating in the universe you didn't know about. In fact, it opens doors to realizing that the potential of man is far greater than we ever imagined, in the sense that it is not limited by time and space.

Many people are having psychic experiences today. The biggest thing to remember is that you are in control, and that there is nothing to fear. You may see spirals of energy, which is probably your own aura. You may see other beings, hear voices, or get glimpses of the future. Remember that the mind is unlimited, and our job is to begin to expand and integrate all these levels of awareness to bring more joy and fulfillment into living.

Remember to be an open-minded skeptic. Ask for the highest information, the truth, in any experience. If you experience anything that is frightening, remind yourself that love is the law of the universe. You can demand that fearful phenomena leave you, and they will depart. Remember to come from a love space and the fear will totally transform itself into a wonder and eagerness to open more and more levels of self to higher knowledge.

Psychic ability is a natural part of our consciousness, but we should not strive to make these gifts the purpose of our meditation. When they are developed more strongly, we will be able to use them wisely provided we are continuing to meditate and balance the mental, physical and spiritual aspects of our beings.

Out Of The Body Experiences

We all have out of the body experiences, but most of us don't remember them. When we leave the body we go out through one of the chakras or energy centers. It makes a great deal of difference which center you leave from, because the level of the chakra determines the quality of your perceptions. For example, if you left the body through the second or sexual chakra, you would be exposed to a much different level than if you left through the third eye center.

Meditation raises the level of energy so that you can leave the body from a higher vibrational level at night. Reading inspirational materials before going to sleep will also aid you in doing this.

Astral projection means that you are traveling or experiencing on the astral plane, which is the vibrational level closest to the physical. To receive higher teachings you must go to higher levels. So "higher plane projection" is really what we should be interested in.

Some groups and publications offer techniques for conscious out of body experiences. These may be effective for some eager students, but we should remember that when we are ready we will be guided into a conscious experience by our own teachers who walk with us. To force out of body experiences may be a little scary (as I discovered the first time I had one) if we are not prepared spiritually to understand what is happening. It is best to continue in your meditation practice and allow the process to occur naturally as you are able to handle it.

Meditation And Psychic Ability

Psychic ability and psychic experiences are often intensified through the process of meditation. This is a normal result of raising your vibrational level. You at first tap into the astral realm, which is beyond the time-space world. But if your purpose is just to gain these powers, ask yourself, "Why do I want this? Will it help me grow in love and awareness? Will it help me serve others?"

Questions And Answers With Dr. William Tiller And The Channel

In the early seventies I asked my channel questions about the nature of psychic phenomena and a variety of other topics in the parapsychology spectrum. On a separate occasion we asked Dr. William Tiller, a professor in the Department of Materials Science at Stanford University, similar questions concerning his experience and beliefs. He had been working with me conducting acupuncture experiments in an effort to understand the flow of healing energy in the body.

Dr. Tiller, an eminent physicist who had just returned from a trip to the Soviet Union to investigate psychic research there, has published hundreds of scientific reports. He has a growing interest in understanding mind, consciousness, time, energy, and how it all relates to a unified theory of man in the universe.

Although the following interview with Dr. Tiller and my channel was first published in *The Sacred Sword* in 1972, the insights and information are even more timely in the present decade.

Psychic Ability And The Nature Of Time And Space

One of the puzzles in psychic research concerns the nature of time, how some people see or know both future and past events. How would you describe time as it relates to the psychic realm?

(CHANNEL) - Time as you know it matters only on your plane of existence. You accept the sequence of time in order to keep yourselves aligned to the days and the seasons, and to the stages you see in man's life process from infancy to old age. Time provides a point of reference. But it is a schedule which earth dwellers get much too involved in. What time really is, few people understand. For all things have existed and all things will continue to exist throughout eternity.

In actuality, time is a vibratory rate. Time is energy. As with all "things," one can attune himself to the rate of vibration of time and *know* it.

Is this how a psychic is able to see things in the future or in the past?

(CHANNEL) - Psychics for the most part are tapping the astral realm, and there is no time on that level. They may see either future or past events. But picking up predictions is very tricky. There has to be a heavy vibrational rate around a thought form or event in order for it to be pin-pointed. Very few have the ability to interpret correctly the vibrational rates on the astral plane. And if you had this ability, you wouldn't want to spend that much time on the astral.

Few psychics are developed to the point where they can maintain the heightened vibration needed to draw from this realm continuously. Instead, they have flashes, or periods of heightened sensitivity, during which they perceive certain things.

Psychics may pick up facts about another person because they are attuning to the vibrations of that person. The entity's force field, or energy field, carries a life plan within it. Yet again, it is often difficult to determine whether the event is a past, present, or future occurrence in the person's incarnation.

Apparently you see time as a finite energy level. How about space?

(CHANNEL) - Space, like time, is an energy. The clairvoyant who is able to see what is happening in another part of the world at the exact moment it is occurring is attuning to the "space vibration." Or, if the person is able to see entities who are out of the body, one has raised one's rate of vibration to their frequency. You tend to think in terms of objects and people when you talk of attuning to vibrations. Yet the gases which make up the air you breathe have vibratory rates. It is difficult to imagine attuning yourself to the same vibration as "air," much less to another *dimension* called *space.*

Traditional science, of course, has questioned the reality of both clairvoyance and precognition—not to mention some of the other phenomena.

(CHANNEL) - Yes, because the majority of scientists have not understood space and time as energies. There are persons now who do understand this, but their research has not become part of the mainstream of scientific thought. Some has not been revealed.

Are experiments on the nature of time being conducted in the Soviet Union?

(DR. TILLER) - Yes, there are experiments going on at a university in Leningrad. The man conducting these has great ability and a considerable reputation. He looks at time as an energy, and is certainly far away from the general thinking of his colleagues.

What do you personally think about the concepts of time and space?

(DR. TILLER) - My own feeling is that we will eventually learn that space and time are properties of waves at the mind and spirit level, the same way as mass and charge are properties of waves at the electro-magnetic level. What this would mean, then, is that time and space are indeed forms of energy. And that by the use of the mind, one can "deform" space and time and thus control them.

There is much information that seems to be pointing out to us that there are dimensions of the universe we know little about, but that are somehow synchronized with our own. Some of these dimensions have very different space-time coordinates than our familiar Einsteinian frame, and some of them seem to be without the limitations of space or time.

Would you elaborate on these other dimensions of the universe?

(DR. TILLER) - The Russians refer to the "bioplasmic realm." Others speak of the "etheric plane." My feeling is that there are several interpenetrating universes, and within this synchronized regime there are material substances within substances within substances, and so on. So this may mean that we have bodies, energy bodies, which would be unobstructed, without the restraints of time and space.

These are different energies than we know anything about, and they obey different laws. We know basically about one kind of stuff, and at this time evidence is suggestive of perhaps seven different kinds of stuff. There is only enough information to suggest that we start looking very seriously for these new energies.

How would you explain man's relation to time and space, and his ability to extend beyond these?

(CHANNEL) - People allow both time and space to rule their lives. They do not realize they are free from these dimensions. Once they gain a full understanding of these they will not be limited.

People must learn that although they perceive themselves to be in physical bodies, made up of denser matter, they are not prisoners in these bodies. The finer energies within them, their "spirits" are free to go into limitless eternity seeking all knowledge and learning all things. This limitless freedom exists not only for teachers and masters, but for each individual soul.

Why can't men perceive these finer energies now?

(CHANNEL) - Some do. But men receive this understanding only as they are able to use it, and apply it directly to their "24 hour a day" lives. You will never be given more of the teachings than you yourself can grasp within your own framework of understanding.

These apparent limitations of time and space prohibit you from abusing the power which is within you. As you learn to live and experience the higher teachings, you may safely receive more. Your spiritual development is essential to using this power wisely. For if you knew the secret to all energies, and everything is energy, you would be able to control your universe.

This knowledge is open to all persons?

(CHANNEL) - That's correct. Through meditation one can learn to understand and go beyond these limited realms. By going within, knowing yourself, and understanding your potentialities: this is the way to be freed for living in the now of eternity.

Acupuncture And Energy Systems

It seems we are beginning to discover more about some of the inner energy systems of man through acupuncture. What is the present status of acupuncture?

(DR. TILLER) - It shouldn't work according to American medicine. But it is found to be effective according to British, European and Eastern medicine; it works there and has been operating effectively for a long time.

I was in London about a year ago and had acupuncture done. I was suffering from a serious indigestion problem. I went to a doctor, and she demonstrated how acupuncture works. She felt the various pulses on the wrist, then said I had problems with the gall bladder and liver meridians. She then used an instrument which measured indications at various acupuncture points on the body to determine which of these particular circuits were affected. Then she knew where to put the needles, or which points of the body to stimulate. The treatment was completely successful.

What was this instrument she was using?

(DR. TILLER) - The instrument measures the resistance of the skin. We have built one and I am now studying it at Stanford. You will find that the skin resistance is on the order of a couple of million ohms generally. But if you touch an acupuncture point with this instrument you find that the resistance drops to something like 100,000 ohms. The device is designed to give you a signal (a light or a sound) when you've touched a localized point of low resistance.

As we locate these various points we see that they correspond to those on the ancient Chinese charts. So the map is already available. With our present instruments we sometimes identify additional points as well.

79

What is the purpose of the needles? How do they make acupuncture work?

(DR. TILLER) - You can use needles, a chemical stimulus, massage, an electrical impulse, a beam of laser light, or the injection of energy from a psychic. My own postulation of what's going on is that perhaps there is another circulatory system of the body we know nothing about. It might be on a par with the blood, lymph, and nervous systems.

I postulate that anyway, because it brings the whole process out in the open, rather than saying the individual is hypnotized, or it "has something to do with the nerves." And we will find out eventually if it is a fluidic circuit as suggested by the ancient Chinese.

Generally, in the fluid circuits of the body, there are little particles called colloids that flow down the tubules. They are very important energy aspects of the body. Now if the body is in balance, if it is healthy, the little particles will flow regularly and there is no problem because they remain dispersed.

However, if the body is out of balance, then you get a type of coagulation phenomena. We're familiar with this in heart conditions, blood clots, and so on. In any case, these particles agglomerate, and they form a raft that is moving down one of these tubules. We might think of the acupuncture points as stations at which there is an eddy in the stream. So the raft may get hung up, and the fluid piles up behind this blockage, just as it does in a normal stream. Then it takes a greater amount of energy to move the fluid through the stream, so you can develop an imbalance between that limb of the circuit and some other limb of the circuit. That imbalance starts to cause ill health. It diverts energy from certain parts of the body to others and creates environmental conditions in which bacteria can grow. These various disharmonies can manifest in the forms we see as disease.

These are speculated reasons why acupuncture works. But at the moment we don't know. We haven't done a lot of serious studies yet to trace this down.

But acupuncture involves a balancing effect on the body?

(DR. TILLER) - Yes, apparently so. The Russians have found that by measuring the same acupuncture point on both right and left sides of the body they get a certain resistance. If they then turn the electrodes around and measure in the reverse direction, there is the same resistance if the individual is healthy. But if the individual is unhealthy in respect to that gland or area, there is a difference in the resistance. The degree of difference is proportional to the degree of disease.

Some Russian scientists did an experiment in which they used a healer to project energy to a sick person whose circuits were unbalanced. They measured some six or seven points on the patient and on the healer before the experiment. The patient showed an imbalance, the healer did not.

Then after the projection of healing they measured the ill person again, and his differential resistance had decreased, which meant he was getting healthier. The healer's resistance had increased. He seemed to have partially unbalanced his own circuits in order to help balance the patient.

You have tried experiments of your own?

(DR. TILLER) - Yes, we thought we'd do a similar experiment. I had an acupuncture device, and my wife had an abdominal problem. And Betty Bethards was a local healer. The points for my wife's abdomen happened to be on the side of the knees. So I measured from left to right, and from right to left, and got a difference in resistance of about twenty per cent. I measured Betty and there was no difference.

Betty projected healing into the acupuncture points at the knees, and the resistance changed on both of them. But the difference was still there. I said, "Okay, just put it in the one knee." And she did, but the difference increased because I picked the wrong knee!

Betty's channel said it wasn't necessary to put this kind of energy into the knees, but to put it into the back of the neck.

They explained that the body has its own intelligence in terms of knowing where best to use this kind of energy. Betty then projected energy into the back of the neck, and I measured the resistances. They had changed. I measured them daily for about a week and a half. The resistance at these places had doubled in magnitude, which meant the health condition had gone up. Then, there was no longer any differential resistance and the abdominal condition was gone.

The Human Aura

Besides trying to learn more about the energy systems and meridians within the body, work has also been done in connection with the human energy field, or aura. Did you see some of this work in Russia?

(DR. TILLER) - In Russia, and now in this country, there have been experiments with what is called Kirlian photography. It is a high voltage photography for detecting energy leaving the skin. The camera responds to electromagnetic energy, although I think there is much more coming out of the skin than just the electromagnetic. Basically what is thought to happen is that electrons are sucked out of the skin and they move across the air gap. They accelerate, hit molecules, and give off bursts of light. That's what exposes the film.

Under a microscope we can observe flares of energy coming out of the body at acupuncture points. Depending on whether a person is tired, emotionally or mentally excited, the color and energy intensity from these flare points changes. When a healer's hands were photographed as he was projecting healing energy, spots of light appeared from many acupuncture points.

Initially the Russians thought they were seeing what clairvoyants have called the aura, but now they aren't sure exactly what is being recorded. They took a leaf and cut part of it away. When they photographed the remaining part, there was an energy pattern of the *whole* leaf. They suggested this might be related to the lost limb effect when a person loses an arm or leg and still has sensation in the phantom limb.

Two things come to mind. First of all, the main energy they see is cold electron emission coming out of acupuncture points from the leaf. But secondly, this phenomenon suggests that at some deeper level of substance there is a radiation from coherent energy sources which would give rise to a pattern of energy like a hologram. This hologram might provide the force field which allows the organization of matter at a physical level. This matter would take on, or follow, the pattern given from this other level.

Now that's very consistent with our idea of interpenetrating universes.

And this would have significant implications in medicine?

(DR. TILLER) - If this bears out with future experiments, then it implies that if an individual loses a leg the primary energy pattern of the leg will still be there. If we know how to work with this pattern, and feed it cellular material in the right way, then we may indeed be able to grow a new leg just like a salamander can.

Some experiments have been done in which the muscle of a rat was removed, ground up, and then fed back into the open cavity from which the muscle was originally taken. After a few weeks the experimenters found that, in fact, the muscle became reorganized in the appropriate pattern.

So the possibility of working with cellular substances and applying them to organizing energy patterns indeed exists.

How would you describe this energy field, or aura?

(CHANNEL) - The aura is made up of interpenetrating energy fields, and is beyond the electromagnetic range. It consists of what we call bio-energy, the life energy, which you have virtually no concept of at this time.

You'll find that the frequency is as fast as thought, if you can but imagine this, and this is why it has not been photographed with any degree of success. For thought is faster than the speed of light.

Psychokinesis, The Power of Thought

Understanding the power of thought would help us understand how psychokinesis operates?

(CHANNEL) - The psychokinesis experiments going on today are hardly scratching the surface. By way of a comparison, the pyramids were built by this thought process. Rocks were cut out, lifted up, and placed into position by concentrated thought energy from a group in a circle.

What can we hope to learn through the study of pyramids in Egypt?

(CHANNEL) - The pyramids were built in order to preserve the knowledge of the Atlanteans, their secrets for understanding the powerful energies of the universe. Potentially these could destroy the human race. And man is not yet ready spiritually again to discover these secrets.

The pyramids are situated on powerful vibratory fields of the earth plane. There is a vibrant magnetism going up from the earth through the center of the pyramid, and this combined with the forces from the sun and planetary influences gives you a power far stronger than you can imagine. Atlantis was also built on such a field.

Back to psychokinesis as such. Have you seen some experiments?

(DR. TILLER) - In Russia I have seen experiments in psychokinesis. They were impressive. The most impressive example was when I was in a restaurant in Leningrad. Nelya Kulagina came into the restaurant and sat down next to me at my table. There were a number of us there to investigate the

Russian work. She took off her wedding ring and placed it on the table about three or four feet from her. She sat back with her hands clasped and just looked at it. She twisted her head a little bit, and the ring started to move across the table.

Now I am a physicist, brought up on Newtonian physics and Einstein type physics. I found myself having to think that maybe there are some other forces and aspects of physics operative in the universe that we don't know anything about.

I saw another individual who was just learning to move objects. She was able to roll an object. This is an easier task, for it involves only the resistance of rolling friction, whereas the other involves moving a whole mass and overcoming static friction.

What do you think the principle of psychokinesis might be?

(DR. TILLER) - I don't think any of us understands it. From my observation I think the Russians have found that there is an energy manifestation in the vicinity of the object. They found that this energy field pulsates. The respiration rate, the alpha waves, and the heart rhythm of the sender all come into synchronization. And they find that when they move the energy detector from the object towards the sender, they reach a domain where they no longer pick up the energy, almost as if the energy utilizes some other pathway and appears in the vicinity of the object. Now in terms of our conventional physics that's not the way things would operate. I don't think we've even begun to understand what's really happening.

Breakthrough In Telepathy

While you were in Russia, what else did you see that impressed you?

(DR. TILLER) - The telepathy work is impressive. The Russians have done many experiments, some with rabbits. In one such experiment they hooked a mother rabbit up to an encephalograph, then took her babies down under the ocean in a submarine. They killed them, one by one. Every time one was killed a change in the brain pattern of the mother was recorded. This showed that there was a linkage between the children and the mother, and that the transmission of awareness was not by electromagnetic energy.

Do you think that telepathy is fairly common among humans?

(DR. TILLER) - I suspect that there is much more communication of a non-physical nature among people than we realize. A person can be thought of as a radio station operating on a particular band of frequencies and at a particular power level. But the radiation is just not in the electromagnetic spectrum as far as I'm concerned. We've yet to prove that, although there have been experiments where people were put in Faraday cages which should rule out the electromagnetic theory.

Do you relate telepathy to the energy centers, or chakras, of the body?

(DR. TILLER) - Yes, as we get into this we need to consider the Eastern literature and the chakras. The endocrine glands function at a physical level, and I think the chakras are at the next finer level of substance. And these act much like a transducer: they receive, transduct, and then broadcast energy. If you are a high power station you can walk into a room and people will feel it.

Artificial Reincarnation

What else is going on in the Soviet Union that you found particularly interesting?

(DR. TILLER) - Perhaps the work on what is called "artificial reincarnation." This is a form of dynamic hypnosis in which you suggest to people that they are principal figures from the past and they take on the characteristics of those figures. You can take an individual who plays the piano only adequately, who is interested and does a bit of training. Under this type of hypnosis you can suggest that he is a famous concert pianist. The transformation one sees in his ability is really great. Professionals themselves say he is playing like a professional.

When you take the individual out of this state of consciousness, he has this increased ability to some degree, but it fades after about five days. If you continue to have the individual practice during this five day period, and alter his state of consciousness back and forth, between the normal and the hypnotized state, then you can transfer some of this ability to his normal consciousness. You can keep taking a person into this hypnotic state, and then out, and over a period of about a year his ability to perform with these talents may increase ten to one hundred fold.

I saw the work of a young girl who had been a physics student, and not particularly interested in art. By using this technique, suggesting that she was a famous artist, she was drawing at the level of commercial artists at the end of a year. In fact, she was thinking of changing her profession.

This says quite a lot about the power of thought.

(DR. TILLER) - Yes, in essence we could all be great with respect to a particular talent. Now I think we can do this with ourselves just by self-suggestion. It's done with our own mind! We can tap that level of consciousness that contains the ability, and make it consciously ours.

Directions In Psychic Research

After having been to Russia, would you say that their research is generally ahead of that in other countries?

(DR. TILLER) - First of all, it's very hard to say how far ahead of us they are. Much of it is underground. But that which we've seen is fantastic.

I know that they have been working on it very strongly since about 1960, after Stalin's death. And, of course, they did a lot of good work back in the thirties. Now it's government sponsored.

I think we saw just a little bit of the iceberg. So I can't really make any comparisons.

What specific area do you think psychical research should pursue now?

(CHANNEL) - The importance of psychical research at this particular time lies in bringing science and religion together. Once science accepts *survival* of the soul, a new harmony will emerge. A new understanding of the universal laws and how matter and energy are combined to work together will result.

But right now some researchers have abandoned experiments which try to prove survival beyond physical death because of the difficulty in establishing such proof.

(CHANNEL) - This is very true. Right now researchers are using mediums who are going to the astral level and contacting entities. Much of the information is unreliable. This is not where you are going to find your proof of survival. Your proof must come from an understanding of the energy field which is within you, from finding out that you are not limited to this body. By being able to establish proof of this energy field, you will know it is *that* which goes on.

Interest Today In Psychic Phenomena

Why do you think there is such a keen interest in psychic phenomena today?

(CHANNEL) - You are moving into a period where the expansion of awareness is being accelerated for many people, and they are experiencing psychic happenings. Unfortunately, if they have not been meditating, they will not know how to control this energy, or they will control but misuse it. The veil between physical and etheric worlds is thinning, and it is very important that people learn how to use wisely these new sensitivities.

How do you as a scientist account for the growing interest in psychic phenomena today?

(DR. TILLER) - I think it's worth saying that at this point in time it appears that there is an increase in this kind of energy in the universe. Therefore, many people are picking up this energy. It's moving in their organism and they don't understand it. They have feelings they don't understand and so they are frightened. And they try to block it. But trying to block this energy is like having a cat loose inside of you. This energy is going to build up in certain places and then discharge through the body. It will probably be through some aspect of the nervous system, and could "burn off" some of the insulation, so to speak.

If one keeps going on in this way, he begins to have uncontrolled fear. The body may begin to do things the individual didn't intend for it to do, and one moves toward a type of schizophrenia. I think many people today are suffering from this. In fact, their own weaknesses start being accentuated. It is mainly because there is an energy in the system that people don't know how to work with or how to use.

Meditation And Spiritual Man

How Can They Learn To Use This Energy?

(DR. TILLER) - Meditation makes you increasingly more coherent in terms of passage of energy through your body. You can actually function with much greater energy in both your day-to-day business and family life and in the "extra" sensory aspects of your life.

But one can have a sense of imbalance with meditation as well. If an individual starts meditation and does it virtually all day long, then his life becomes very unbalanced and he no longer works in the "real" world.

Meditation can be used in a passive sense to merely escape from the turmoil and stresses of the physical world we live in (and many use it this way). Or, it can be used in a dynamic sense to enhance perception, regenerate vitality, and focus attention on coherent courses of action to resolve the seeming dilemmas of the physical world around us; that is, it makes us more capable of effective action.

Generally, meditation is beneficial to one when he oscillates between the state of consciousness associated with the external world and his work there, because that's where he tests his responses, and then oscillates back into this altered state of consciousness in meditation. It is here that you will sense the wide panorama of your inner life, in my judgment, and integrate or bring continuity to the total self.

So practicing meditation helps one understand psychic energy. How is the psychic actually related to "spiritual" man?

(CHANNEL) - Psychic ability really has nothing to do with spirituality. Many people have psychic sensitivity but are spiritually unaware.

Spirituality can grow from this psychic ability if the person comes to realize that the universe offers much more than he or she had ever imagined.

The psychic energy is certainly a higher frequency than the average man is able to use. But the spiritual energy, or realm, is a qualitatively different dimension.

Mystics as well as psychics claim to experience a realm beyond time. How would you describe a mystic, and what is he experiencing?

(CHANNEL) - A mystic is an entity who looks strictly to the Universal Intelligence, to God, for answers. The mystic may move freely within the seven planes. This is why one will have the highest visions, and experience the most profound truths. The mystic is beyond any enchantment with phenomena.

This state of awareness comes through many incarnations of working in the occult (which is a lower form), in healing, and in channeling. Mysticism is the elite of gifts or achievements. The true mystical experience is the closest thing to Nirvana.

Can you describe Nirvana?

(CHANNEL) - It defies description. Simply, it is a peace, an attunement to all forces. You may move freely throughout the planes of the universe. You have the ability to know the beauty within each soul, no matter what plane of life it is on.

Would you say that Nirvana corresponds to having all the chakras open and controlled?

(CHANNEL) - No. Many people have their chakras open, or have the crown chakra open, but still do not know what Nirvana is. It is a qualitatively different state of energy attunement.

Many are highly illuminated, but have not yet experienced this. Many masters today claim to have done so, but there are, in fact, only a handful on the earth plane who have experienced it.

Earlier you mentioned that man, potentially, is able to control time. And it is said that "spiritual" people often appear ageless.

(CHANNEL) - People who are meditating slow down the aging process. They often retain a youthful look, due to the high vibrations within them. For meditation actually changes every cell in the body.

Sorrow, misery and unhappiness are part of what causes you to age. If you were at peace and harmony within yourself, you would not age nearly so quickly.

How do you think meditation might be related to the time process, or to health?

(DR. TILLER) - I feel that meditation does, indeed, change the cells in one's body, for it is a harmonizing process. It literally can have a rejuvenating effect.

The Russians have shown, for example, that if you project negative thoughts to an individual you can decrease the white cell count of the body. By sending positive thoughts you can increase the white cell count, hence the person would tend to have immunity to disease.

Thought, meditation, can indeed affect the bodily processes.

It would seem, then, that we have only begun to realize what some of the vast potentialities of man might be. In closing, do you have any counsel as to the most effective way to continue exploration of the psychic— and other—realms?

(CHANNEL) - As you continue to explore the psychic dimension and beyond, you will discover that understanding must be integrally related to the evolution of your own consciousness.

Meditation is the process which regulates and speeds up this evolution, for it attunes you to the finer energies of the universe. When you understand the powerful forces within, you will know the reality behind all phenomena, all things.

Chapter 5:

Meditation: Way To The Guru Within

Meditation And Self Growth

The heart of my message to people is meditation. It doesn't matter whether I'm talking about healing, reincarnation, prosperity, sex and psychic energy, or improving communications. Everything stems from an awareness of self. The only way we can grow, improve our lot in life, is through changing our inner perspective.

Meditation, besides putting us in touch with the God center of our beings, the Guru within, has an obvious effect on our daily lives. We find that we develop a growing sense of serenity, become more and more free from anxieties, frustrations, and hostilities. We are more tuned in to ourselves, and so we are more tuned in to others. Our overall sense of communication improves.

People and situations which formerly made us uptight don't bother us as much anymore. We are inclined to be more understanding toward others, and we think more about life's meaning and direction. Our minds seem clearer, our health improves.

No two persons will have exactly the same results from meditation, however, for each person's needs are unique. Each of us has to work out our specific problems in this lifetime. We may expect meditation to put us in touch with our tasks and to help us advance toward their fulfillment.

Although some positive benefits are experienced almost immediately, such as the peacefulness during the meditation period itself, many changes are gradual and you may hardly be aware of them. Meditation is not a wonder drug that magically cures all our ills overnight. It does begin to sensitize us to the problems at hand and heighten our energy level so that we can grow faster and move through whatever is facing us. In time we will become aware that we are very different people than when we first started the meditation process.

Belief Is Not Important

You do not have to think of yourself as religious to practice meditation. Anyone can meditate, because it does not depend upon what you believe. You don't even have to believe in the value of meditation itself. Whatever your religious belief, it can enhance your faith. If you are a healthy skeptic this is probably to your benefit, because you will recognize the unique changes that occur within, minus any expectations on your part.

Meditation is not an end in itself, and this is important to remember. It is a process, a means to establishing your inner connection.

What is needed as you begin is open-mindedness and a commitment to spend at least twenty minutes a day in meditation. No one can meditate for you. All the talking about it and reading about it will not change you. You simply have to do it. Sometimes it is helpful to arrange to meditate with a group of people at least once a week, because this provides additional support and motivation. When the Foundation first started teaching meditation, we sponsored hundreds of free meditation groups. At that time, however, meditation was still a new idea to many people, and those who practiced it were considered a little weird. Group support was especially important. But whether you prefer to meditate with a group or on your own, remember your growth is entirely up to you.

94

After you've been meditating for awhile you
benefits even more when you skip a day or two
drops, and things just don't seem to go as well. T
more faithfully you've been meditating the more y
difference. Your energy field becomes accustome. .o getting
its recharge every twenty-four hours, and when it doesn't it
seems scattered.

Raising The Kundalini

When you meditate you are raising your kundalini, or God
energy, which is housed in the base of the spine. This energy
begins to flow upward into all your major energy centers,
recharging them and building your aura.

Your energy centers are located at the base of the spine, in
the sexual organ area, the solar plexus, heart, throat,
forebrain or third eye, and on the crown of the head. The idea
is to gradually awaken all the centers, and learn to function
primarily from the upper ones. For the higher the center, the
clearer the perception.

As you build your aura by bringing through the love energy,
you are not only helping yourself, but are also helping those
around you. They feel and respond to your light.

Meditation, then, on a daily basis is a way of recharging
yourself, building your energy field. In this way you are able to
see things clearer around you and stay detached from
problems in order to solve them more effectively. When your
energy is down you can't see anything clearly, for the whole
world looks like its against you. But as we learn to build our
energy and maintain it we protect ourselves from negativity,
illness, and confusion. It's a great way to go!

Transcending Dimensions

Over the longer haul meditation heightens awareness so
that you are able to transcend dimensions in your consciousness and perceive higher and higher truths. You easily move

and out of physical awareness, or out of the body, during your meditation period. This is what completely frees you from the fear of death, because you become comfortable functioning on the higher planes, and realize that you are not confined to the physical. You begin to see and hear with the spiritual senses, and discover that you truly are unlimited. Thus meditation heightens your creative ability, and releases talents and abilities that you may not have ever known you had.

If it sounds exciting, it is. The rewards are tremendous. But we must want it enough to spend twenty minutes a day practicing the technique.

The Meditation Technique

The Inner Light Foundation method of meditation is simple but powerful. Meditation is a deep relaxation of body, mind and spirit. It should be done on a daily basis for twenty minutes at whatever time best suits your schedule. The easiest way to meditate is to listen to your favorite songs and music. While sitting with your spine erect, you are aligning to the God Force.

1. Sit in a chair with your spine erect, shoulders relaxed, feet flat on the floor. Fold your hands together in your lap and close your eyes.
2. Take three slow, deep breaths, exhaling to the base of your spine, and feel yourself relaxing. Sit with your hands together for ten minutes.
3. After ten minutes, open your hands, palms up, laying them gently in your lap. Keep your focus on the songs and music.
4. At the end of this ten minute period, when your energy is at its highest, most centered point, you can do your affirmations and visualizations, such as "The perfect career is manifesting in my life now," or whatever you are

choosing to create in your life, i.e., wisdom, ⌐
perity. If your buttons were jammed during the
can review the situation, see what your positive lessε
and visualize how you would have liked to have handΙ. Λ.
This way, next time it comes up, as it will until the lesson is
learned, you will handle it with love.

5. After completing your affirmations and visualizations, close
your hands into a fist and feel a balloon of white light one
block around you so that you're in the center. This sends
love and healing out to the masses and buffers all negativity from coming in to you.

This twenty minute period, however, is not our only meditation practice. We endeavor to practice the meditation attitude,
watching our thoughts and behavior, throughout each day.
Meditation will also help you get a recall on your dreams. It is
your greatest free tool for self-growth and self-understanding.
Meditation can thus help us to be more fully involved in life
because we can watch how we set up our experiences.
Sometimes changes are subtle and sometimes dramatic.
Meditation does change your life because it changes you.

Learning To Trust The Guru Within

As we continue in our meditation we may be exposed to
many ideas and given many teachings. We may ask for
answers to problems or insights in relationships. One of the
continuing questions is: How can I trust what I get? You may
ask for insight, and you may imagine that a teacher appears
and discusses the problem with you. (In fact, this is a very
helpful guided meditation technique. Picture a very wise being
talking to you, and listen to what this being is saying.)

Often you feel like whatever you hear or see in meditation
you are making up. We are hesitant to trust information that
comes to us from this level. This is good, because it never pays

to be gullible. You may get great truths, or your own fears and desires may get in the way and you get a lot of distortions.

The guiding principle to use is always the same, as I mentioned earlier: take what feels right and chuck the rest. If you get a message that makes a lot of sense to you and it is loving, then it is probably a good idea to listen to it. But if a being in a long white robe appears and tells you something that you don't feel is right for you, then forget it. We always have to make our own decisions, come to terms with our own problems. We should never blindly follow what anyone else suggests we do, whether they are in or out of the body.

The Guru (or God) within is really your own intuition. Knowledge comes to you in a strong, positive sense of knowing something is true. The higher you raise your energy through meditation, the more accurate your intuitive sense will be. The more you practice detachment, learning to release other people and situations to their highest good rather than trying to control things, the clearer you will be, also. Again, there is an old saying: The man who has no preferences has no trouble seeing truth. This doesn't mean we should have no goals, no plans in life. But it does mean that when we ask for guidance in a certain situation we should really desire the best for all concerned, recognizing the higher spiritual energies guiding everyone's life. We limit our understanding when we are attached to specific results or outcomes. If we really let things go, desiring nothing but the best, something better than what we could have anticipated will always come about. It is our attachment, our fear, that prevents us both from seeing and from experiencing the fullness of life.

Problems In Meditation

Meditation cannot possibly be dangerous or harmful. It can only result in good, for the whole orientation or direction is toward the love force, or God. But it is helpful to remember that when you begin meditating you are accelerating your own growth. Sometimes negativity which you have suppresssed may surface, because it is time to look at it. You have to let it come up and out. Don't stop meditating because negative thought forms are floating through your consciousness.

Again, the whole key is detachment. What you are experiencing is just an experience. A negative pattern of thought or behavior is not you, but just a program that you adopted as your own. It is these very programs that limit our awareness of the God self. So if you don't want to really get to know the self, the beauty that is under all that garbage you've been hoarding, then don't start meditating. Just realize that the garbage does have to get emptied, and you can make a little game of it. "Oh boy, here comes another one!" "Thanks, God, I really appreciate this nice opportunity for growth." "What's a nice person like me doing with a thing like that?!"

There may be what we could call other pitfalls to meditation. You may not see results as rapidly as you would like, get discouraged, and give up. Or, you could go on an ego trip thinking that you are better than others and must really have it together now that you're meditating.

Some people experience definite sensations during meditation and become frightened because they do not understand them. Perhaps its a sudden rush of energy up the spine, a feeling of a breeze on your face, or tingling in your hands. Or you may begin to rock gently back and forth during the meditation phase.

If you see or hear anything that you don't like, whether it appears in the form of a thought or being, you can always say, "Go to progression." This means you are telling the image to progress to a higher level and to leave your consciousness alone.

Remember that whatever you are experiencing, you are always in control. You can at any time break the meditation flow by simply closing your palms and opening your eyes. There is nothing to fear, for fear is within us and can be looked at directly whenever it surfaces. Whenever we face what we fear it immediately dissipates.

Also, during the first several years of meditating remember not to overdo it. Keep your meditation periods in moderation. Meditating too much and too long and possibly neglecting your karmic tasks will not result in the kind of growth you expect. What you learn in short meditation periods should be tested in your daily life. Don't try to escape from life by running to meditate.

Meditation And Healing

Healing is a complex process. In general it involves bringing about vibrational harmony among all aspects of the self: spirit, mind, and body. Meditation is an attunement process, and thus it is also a healing process.

People who seriously undertake meditation are likely to experience an increase in vitality and a general improvement in health. Specific symptoms are likely to disappear.

People who meditate regularly may soon feel an energy flow from their fingertips which is the healing power. They will learn to become channels through which this healing energy can flow to their fellows. In meditation groups this healing power may be greatly multiplied. It may be directed to a member of the group or to someone absent.

Do not hesitate to send out healing thoughts, even if you think you are not sufficiently developed to do so. Vividly *picture* the person well and active, the healing power of love surrounding him or her. You can do this any time during the day, or at the close of your meditation when your energy is the highest.

Disease actually results from an imbalance within the physical, mental, and spiritual self. There would be no disease if people could keep their energy level high and all three of these aspects going as a balanced whole. Disease is a disharmony of the vibrations.

Meditation as a healing process involves changing the rate of vibration of whichever element of the self is out of harmony. That is why if one receives a healing from another person, and

100

is not meditating to keep the vibrations high and aligned, sickness will return again.

Healing is not some sort of magic, but is rather a continuing process. Maintaining a state of good health is our individual responsibility, and this can best be done on a daily basis through our meditation attunement.

Each one of us is a channel for the healing energy, and the strongest level of this energy is love. We should always send love or healing energy to others, whether we think their illness is terminal or temporary. This energy can help to bring about a healing of some if not all aspects of the self, or aid spiritual insight.*

Dreams, Prayer And Meditation

I have often commented that the only three tools we need to get through life are absolutely free: dreams, prayer, and meditation.

Dreams play a vital part in developing spiritual awareness. Primitive cultures understood dreams as the self actually leaving the body and having the experiences dreamed about. And they were mostly on the right track. In most dreams one is not literally having the experience, but the dream is a symbolic representation of a process occurring within one or more levels of consciousness.

The conscious mind is out of the way when you're asleep. The subconscious is like a storage bank which contains all experiences of this lifetime—both in and out of the body. The superconscious goes way beyond. It is like the God self, is totally detached, and looks at what is going on.

Dreams may occur, however, on many levels. We all definitely leave the body at night to receive higher teachings. Sometimes we remember these in the form of dreams and sometimes we do not. A dream may seem like a jumbled

*For an in-depth look at the healing process, see *Techniques for Health and Wholeness.*

message of nothing important, which could reflect our scattered energy from the day. Or the dream may be profound, giving new creative ideas, direction, or glimpses of the future.

How we tune in to our dreams, how seriously we take them, determines to a large extent what we will receive. If we carefully watch our dreams, especially if we meditate before going to bed to clear out most of the trivia, then we will begin to get some fascinating and very helpful material. Dreams give us an honest daily reading on where we are blowing it, what we need to work on, what we have completed, what is happening in relationships, and so on.

When we gain greater control of the dream state, regularly remembering our dreams, we can begin to use dreams for problem solving. Getting control of the dream state is a great step in opening ourselves to expanded realms of knowledge. We have all heard the statement, or perhaps we have made it ourselves, that we are going "to sleep on it." We are going to sleep on some problem or situation, and usually the next morning we awaken sensing the answer.

The dream level is another equally real level of consciousness, and since we are not able to screen out information with our rational minds we are open to much greater insights and experiences. To begin to get in touch with this level, first begin to remember and record your dreams. Get yourself a good dream book and familiarize yourself with some of the main symbols (although each person must determine the meaning of individual symbols which appear in dreams.) And definitely continue with your meditation. Many of the dream images begin to appear also in the meditation state, and you begin to build bridges of awareness from one level to the next. Remember that meditation enables you to integrate the many levels of consciousness so that you may draw power and insight from the total self.

Prayer is the formulation in your mind of what it is that you want or need. God already knows what we want, but if we don't then we aren't going to be able to manifest it. Prayer is really getting clear within yourself. It should not be thought of as supplication to a whimsical God who may grant your wish if He or She is in the right mood. Prayer is really asking your higher self to direct you, to guide you, or stating very clearly what it is you feel would best help your growth at this time.

I have often heard people say that prayer doesn't work. It certainly does if we expect results. Most of us ask for things in our lives and have no real feeling that they will actually happen. Doubts surround our statements of request, and so we undermind ourselves. But we should always remember to add whenever we pray for things, especially if they are material things or relationships: "This or something better, as it is Your will." Remember the old adage, "Be careful what you ask for. You might get it." We may not know within the rational mind what is really best for our growth, and so we should include a corrective. Don't be attached to the specifics. Remember that the ways of God, Universal Mind, are magnificent and unknown to the little rational mind of man.

So meditation helps us get in touch with the Guru within, heighten our awareness and recharge our energy fields. Prayer helps us to formulate our goals, clarify our needs and the direction for our life. Dreams give us daily out of the body experiences, and daily readings on what's happening in our lives. They also provide a door to the intuitive so that we may get insight on any problem we are facing, new creative ideas to enhance our lives, and higher teachings from the other side.

Meditation And Sleep

The spiritual masters have long known that the more time they spent in meditation, the less sleep they needed. The physical body needs sleep to rejuvenate and rebuild itself, to relax tension and to have a reprieve from the conscious mind. But this process is accelerated if body, mind, and spirit are first harmonized through meditation. Thirty minutes of meditation may substitute for two or three hours of sleep.

Physical sleep alone will not replenish the energy needed for the harmonious working together of the physical-mental-spiritual self. If worry and fear prevent you from relaxing, you will wake up tired the next morning. This is one reason that meditation just before bedtime is helpful. You attune all aspects of yourself so that your whole being may be renewed, and that you will be more receptive to the teaching you receive during sleep.

The soul, the real you, does not need physical sleep. Consequently, when the body is at rest, *you* are taken from the body and taught on the higher planes.

Meditation And Emotional Control

If you feel you are on an emotional yoyo in life, swinging up and down and unable to control your moods, your energy is not high and balanced. In fact, a high percentage of the population experience this, most being emotional eight to ten year olds. My channel has said that this is helpful to keep in mind when dealing with others: a fifty year old may in fact be an emotional 10 year old and will act accordingly under stress.

Most of us never received emotional development training. It is not part of the educational system. Yet before we can complete our tasks on the earth plane we must have achieved emotional balance. The best way to do this is through meditation, which raises the energy and harmonizes the energy field. But first let us understand what emotions actually are.

My channel has explained that emotion is a force, an expression of energy. Emotions or feelings are ways of perceiving things. As energy they can be experienced through the higher or lower chakras. When they are experienced primarily through the lower chakras, we are on a reactionary level. We get sucked into other people's trips and cannot stay objectively and lovingly removed.

Once you get energy above the fifth chakra all things are seen as positives. Nothing is experienced as stressful, or separated into categories of good and evil. Emotions are windows to a deeper level of intuitive knowing, and when elevated to higher awareness actually get translated into intuition. Since most people on the earth plane are operating from the second chakra (sexual) or third chakra (solar plexus), they experience emotions as feelings of separateness, passion, struggle, possessiveness, have great highs and lows, and are not in control of this force.

In the second chapter we talked about programs. It is within the lower emotional level that all the programs we are running on ourselves come out: fears, insecurities, and so on.

The reason positive programming doesn't seem to work for some people is because they are not combining it with meditation. They want to change their old programming but their energy is not high enough to maintain a new perspective. This we see happening to us when we get tired, when our energy is down. Things which normally don't bother us drive us up the wall. People we love and care about seem to irritate us just by being there.

Another good example of how energy affects our perspective and ability to deal with problems is that often, once we are actually centered in the meditation process, we can't seem to remember what the problem was that seemed so urgent. We enter our meditation period with the idea that we want to solve it. When our energy is raised all the old feelings, programs and trips that we get trapped in fade away because we have elevated our energy and perceptual levels. What has happened is that the energy is being experienced more through the heart and higher centers, rather than the lower chakras.

To grow beyond the lower emotional level we must be very honest with ourselves and look at what we are experiencing, just as we must do with negative programs. This does not mean that we are taking feeling and spontaneity out of our lives. The emotions are a lower form of energy that greatly limit our awareness. Love and creativity are forms of the higher chakra expressions of this same energy. Creativity is anything but boring: it is spontaneity in its essence! What limits our creativity now is the fear and other negativity that we process through ourselves, the lower emotions.

But isn't love an emotion, you might ask? On the lower emotional scale what we call love is really an effort to be accepted by others and to validate our own egos. We may occasionally rise above this. But the quality of love that manifests through a higher awareness has nothing to do with possessiveness, manipulation, wanting to change others, or wanting to get ego strokes.

Negative Emotions

Our negative emotions show us the very things we need to work on. Fear is the primary negative emotion, all others stemming from it. The basic lesson with fear is we must face what we fear.

We should learn to walk up to our fears with arms outstretched, welcoming the lesson it has brought us. When we see these fear programs as teachers to help us grow, we can actually project a feeling of love and thankfulness toward them. The only reality a fear has is what we have momentarily invested in it. As soon as we are able to say, okay, I want to know what you are teaching me, the whole fear energy changes. It is back under our control. We look at it, learn from it, and then it disappears.

One of the biggest fears is fear of failure. To overcome this we must learn to understand that the purpose of life is to grow, to progress. We make mistakes, but this is in order to help ourselves and our fellows.

Don't be afraid of falling flat on your face. You'll learn how not to do something. To accomplish any task set before you, proceed with all your strength of purpose and with a positive attitude. Whatever the outcome, you will have gained strength and knowledge and this will serve you at a later time.

One of the other most useless emotions is guilt. Guilt is based on ignorance of the law of karma. It is rooted in fear, and like any negative emotion must be overcome. Guilt is a big one, especially because so many religions have fostered it as a way to control the people.

Feeling guilty, we seek forgiveness, which means we want someone to erase the consequences of what we do. But no one can do this for us. We must change our own way of thinking, our actions, through learning from our mistakes. Our desire for forgiveness often implies a lack of trust in a universal, caring force. We search for pardon thinking that an outside God is vindictive. We are always forgiven, but we must still accept the responsibility for our actions and grow from them. You can't hurt anyone unless he or she sets you up to do it. If you weren't available they would have found someone else to jam their button.

In religious scriptures the idea of forgiveness mainly concerns the importance of ridding the self of guilts, freeing the self. If you are hung-up in your own guilts, you cannot be aware of the needs of your fellows. You must put these guilts and fears aside, and dwell only on your strengths.

All people have hurt others, have hated, have acted violently, in one incarnation or another. No one is free from the pangs of growth through the earth plane. Thus, as you learn to see yourself as part of the whole human life wave, you feel the struggles, the joys, and the frustrations of all people. When you truly learn to accept the responsibility of your own thoughts, words and deeds, you are filled with compassion and love for all people.

One of the greatest things to remember when dealing with the emotions is a sense of humor. A sense of humor is very important in overcoming your fears, your negative feelings. Being able to laugh at your own mistakes has an uplifting, balancing effect. When you are depressed, very often you fail to see the lesson you were meant to learn. But if you can laugh and look at the situation lightheartedly, the lesson will shine through and you will grow beyond it.

Meditation As Total Communication

Meditation is a way to know your whole being, to communicate with all dimensions of yourself, to see yourself as an unlimited expression of the God energy. To communicate with yourself is to know yourself, and when you know yourself you know all things. The following channeling is on meditation as a communication process.

You may best develop a total communication with yourself, with others and with God by knowing yourself. If you don't know yourself, of course, how could you know your destiny, main purpose in life, or what you are supposed to be working on?

You must take responsibility for setting your own goals in life. The idea is to take control of your life, get at the helm of your ship, chart your voyage and head for that goal. There is no way you can fail. Whatever you do you can learn from it.

But today so many of you are setting your vessels adrift on a lonely sea. You think, "Wherever I happen to wind up is all right." But a captain must have a chart, a map, to make it to a destined shore. How often do you find yourself in a situation and say, "Well, God must mean for me to be here." But does God mean for you to be there? Suddenly you have put all the responsibility for your lack of taking charge and developing self-insight on God.

But you must take charge, you must determine your destiny. Dare to go after what you want. Set your goals and once you obtain them set more. This is the only way they can manifest. No one from this side or the earth plane can do it for you. Take the helm and guide your ship. Chart your own way. Use the stars to guide you but follow your own heart.

The only way to develop insight into yourself, hence insight into your relationships with others and your purpose in life, is through your daily meditation. All the programs that have been running in your head for lifetimes you think are reality. You project these programs on others which muddles your awareness and on your own self-image which distorts and limits your abilities.

As you open to the Guru within, the captain of your ship, the Knower within your soul, a new and higher level of perception fills your awareness. An inner sense of joy and love begin to guide you to your perfect fulfillment, because you are becoming aware of all dimensions of your being.

It is only as you know the self that you are truly able to help others. It is only through your daily meditation that you learn to love yourself, accept yourself, and permit your true potential to unfold.

Chapter 6:

The Promise
Of Our Age

The Potential For Everything

We are living in an exciting period of history. In fact, *it is the best time to be in the body!* The Age of Aquarius holds great promise for all mankind, yet it also presents many challenges that must be met if we are to get through these next several decades.

We see all around us the very best and the very worst of human behavior. This creates turmoil and confusion in the minds of most people, and underlines why it is so important to stay centered through meditation. We see nations at war with one another or arming themselves to the teeth, and see men and women working around the clock to promote peace and avoid nuclear conflict. We see the technology available to produce enough food to feed the world, and yet we see people starving in almost every country. We see great universities and spiritual teachers available to us for learning and growth, and yet ignorance, prejudice, fear, and man's inhumanity to man seem to be soaring.

The potential for whatever kind of a world we want is right here. We can work to create a world of balance and responsibility, or we can go our separate ways, tuning out the problems, and slowly watch our society be destroyed.

This is an age in which we are supposed to learn to know ourselves, and how to effect positive changes within ourselves, our country and our world. This is a time when we have to learn how to do it with love, because the old violence and power trips just won't work anymore. It is not a back to nature age in which we should reject all those things which technology has enabled us to experience.

God has given to every soul the potential and the tools to be rich, loved, healthy, to experience total fulfillment. To learn how to handle material things is a great test of responsibility. Poverty is easy, but it takes a wise man to understand the right relationship between creating things and using them responsibly in one's life to build a world of peace.

Time Of Transition

This is a time of great testing, but also a time of breakthrough. This time of transition for our world means several things. First, as I said, the old ways of dealing with problems aren't going to work any more. We have exhausted our attempts at negative problem solving. Overcoming other peoples and nations through power, through wars, maintaining supremacy based on military might, these levels of dealing with conflict have now reached their absurd limits. We are all aware that the fate of the planet rests with the pushing of a button, that at any time our country or the Soviet Union could launch more than enough missiles and other destructive devices to wipe out civilization, and leave this planet uninhabitable for perhaps thousands of years. Hatred and fear taken to their limits become pure absurdity. We are now seeing this all too clearly: hatred destroys. It's pretty simple.

So, if the old ways have reached their ridiculous proportions, what else is left? My channel has explained that the forces around the earth plane are changing into a spiritual vibration. The veil between the physical and etheric worlds is becoming much thinner. More and more people will begin to have psychic experiences, become interested in meditation, and generally be awakened to higher realms of understanding. The energies are becoming finer and higher. We have an accelerated opportunity to open to new dimensions of understanding. In other words, we have an opportunity to get it together, and not destroy ourselves as we are certainly capable of doing.

This opportunity, whether we take advantage of it, will depend entirely upon our level of inner awareness, developing the spiritual dimensions within us, rather than staying on a materialistic level, operating from the lower chakras.

My channel has said that we are sitting on a time bomb. If we continue abusing the earth, ignoring the ecological balance, if we continue abusing our fellows, and fail to develop the potential within us, we will have little chance of survival on this planet.

The current problem of polution, for example, represents part of the struggle of this particular age. We have abused the earth ever since we've been on it.

Because of the larger population now we are beginning to see the fruits of such misuse. People will have to become aware that they are destroying the very things they need for survival.

Uncontrolled population growth, limited food production, contaminated water supply, smog-ridden cities—lack of awareness has created problems in these and many other areas. Generally we have adopted the attitude, "Live for today and to hell (literally) with tomorrow."

But mind pollution is the originator of the outer manifestations. The ideas with which we saturate ourselves appear in outward form. Our fanatical beliefs, ignorance, and selfishness all have created a pollution within ourselves. This must be cleaned up first if we are to harmonize the forces of the earth.

Atlantis Revisited

The significance of this period lies mainly in its karmic ties with earlier civilizations. Not only do individuals have their separate karma to work out, but so do groups and countries. There are many levels to which we are tied. Particularly important for the United States is its karmic tie with the lost continent of Atlantis. Although this may sound a little kooky, my channel has often spoken of Atlantis and its importance in our problems today. Many of the secrets of Atlantis can still be found in the pyramids of Egypt, they have explained, but we are not yet ready to uncover them.

During the time of Atlantis we were faced with the same choices we have today: work together and recognize that the world is one family, or go our separate ways and continue abusing our resources and power until we collapse. In Atlantis most people did not elevate their energy to the higher chakras, and were operating mainly out of the lower chakras. These, of course, are those through which we see ourselves as separate from others and in which suppression results in violence and the striving for power.

Many people to whom I give readings are former Atlanteans, because a high percentage have now reincarnated. The level of U.S. technological development, though not yet as great, is beginning to approximate that of the ancient civilization. Also, the general period of war and hostility we are witnessing is similar to what they experienced.

The Atlanteans were highly developed intellectually, yet they adopted inhumane laws and practices. They became materialistic, negative and hostile in their relations with one another. They chose not to unite in harmony, and due to both mental and technological disasters their continent was destroyed.

Our conditions today, again, are similar to the conditions or vibrations in Atlantis. In Atlantis we blew it, and I say "we" because many of us were on the earth plane at that time. We are back to see whether we can make it work this time. Can we learn to live in love rather than hatred and fear? Can we really progress into a unified planet?

If we don't make it, if we blow ourselves up again, then we will have to work our way back through time and space, until the vibrations are again the same as we would have left them. We would have to wait until the conditions on the earth plane were again identical, and then we could reincarnate and do the

114

job we have neglected this time. We must eventually work through this karma, and if we are lax now we will return. We can't afford to go off on our own little trips, hoping the problems will disappear. This is not the time in history to seclude ourselves on mountain tops.

What our age calls for is to bring through higher awareness into our everyday lives, to transform the negative into positive, to change the whole level of interaction among men. This sounds like a big order, I know, but we all have a place to begin. This, of course, is within ourselves.

My channel continues to emphasize that we *can* do something about the present situation, that we *can* make our world work and escape the threat of total destruction.

The War Within

"War," guidance has said, "is a result of discord among men who are not at peace with themselves. Man's lack of love for his fellows results in the effort to control others, to exploit others, and to take what is possessed by others. War is the expression of greed, the very opposite of love. War represents man's scattered energies, his illusion of separateness from his fellows. It is the negative state of man's creative energy and power. War embodies hostility, hatred, envy and fear, which are expressions of man's ignorance and misunderstanding."

Think of the hostile thoughts that pass through our individual minds every day. Most of the time we are unaware of them, because they flow in and out with such regularity. They are based, of course, upon our own insecurities. But these hostile vibrations expand into outward reality and we find ourselves saying and doing things that are hurtful to others. War, the outer manifestation of our inner fear, negativity and hatred, can indeed be prevented. But this must be done by individually regulating our thought vibrations. We can never legislate peace into existence. We can never outlaw war effectively until we have first changed ourselves.

We have all heard the saying that conquering one's self is far more significant than conquering a nation. It is also far more difficult. Unless we learn to conquer the self, our own passions and emotions, we have conquered nothing.

Peace, what we are striving for in this present age, represents a state of consciousness attuned to the cosmic consciousness. There is a real and definite level of vibration identified with peace, ultimately more real and powerful than the destructive lower vibrations of hostility and hatred.

We can hope to create a peaceful world, we can make it this time around. If I didn't really believe that I wouldn't be teaching what I'm teaching. When great numbers of people express the love vibration, peace and harmony can be brought to reign among us. But we have to start with ourselves where the problem has its origin. We spread it to others, and they to others, until we begin to get a toehold on creating this world of peace we're talking about.

Peace, Brotherhood And Harmony

The following is a message from the channel on *Peace, Brotherhood and Harmony:*

You ask us to speak on peace and brotherhood. We would add "harmony," for without harmony you cannot develop the other two.

What is peace? Is it outward agreements among nations or between neighbors? No, when people search deeply they discover peace is something which resides in the God-soul. Only when they take time to develop an awareness of peace will they bring this flow of energy into every dimension of their lives.

Without personal peace within the individuals who make up nations, it is not possible for nations to get along with one another. This is important to the success of your own government, your own land. Each of you can learn to feel and to know the peace which resides deep in the soul. If you cannot accomplish this within yourself, you will find it cannot exist without.

116

Peace is a blending of persons in truth and harmony, one with the other. It is seeing the God-nature of every man. It is reaching out and extending to every fellow human being the love force you discover at the center of your own nature.

All are essentially one unit. What is needed is a harmonizing of vibrations, the positive vibrations at the love end of the vibratory scale. If each soul were aware of the peace-love power within, there would be a natural harmony uniting all men in a brotherhood which could withstand all threats. There would not be war or suffering, for men would be free from the greed and hatred that makes them exploit one another.

If you could accept the plan or will of one God, the Cosmic Intelligence, you would see that it intends each of you to find your identity with the God-source and with all fellow creatures. You would know that as you hurt another you hurt yourself. And as you give to another you receive in return. This is the law of karma in action. If you would develop the love power, and learn to express it in your daily living, you would find the brotherhood your world is searching for would actually be.

How tragic is the lack of trust in your land and among the nations! If peace reigned within your hearts, the sorrow and suffering of discord throughout the world would end. This is our whole task, and yours if you will accept it—to encourage love and peace among men.

The task of all mankind is thus essentially a peace-building task. True peace is the God power or love force manifesting through you as you get in touch with your divine nature. There is no way really to serve mankind other than to bring this love force to its fullest potential within your own being.

In brotherhood you will be able to become fully aware of those less fortunate than youself. We do not ask that you give to others material things, although if one is starving or needs shelter he should not be turned away. The greatest gift you can impart to your fellowmen is the teaching that love and peace can flow from their own meditation. You cannot, of course, do it for them—they must learn it themselves. But you can set them on the path and guide them until such time as they are able to know their own inner strength.

It is sometimes very difficult when others are crying out for help to tell them they must do it themselves. It is a big responsibility to live and to transmit the higher teachings to others. It is a task made easier if you call upon the love-source for guidance and knowledge.

It is easier to help a person who knows nothing than a wise man who knows all. For those who "know" only on the mental plane will not be able to set aside their intellect in order to feel and thus to grow on the deeper levels of awareness. It is the lower self which manifests as the logical intellect of mankind. It is emphasis on this to the exclusion of the higher intuitive or feeling self which has brought your nation to the brink of disaster.

There will be times when you will be called upon to help one who is in need who does not offer peace and love in return. It is still important for you to do all in your power to teach the right attitude and to share the knowledge of how to find the way if one should desire to choose it. Whether the other person accepts what you offer is not your responsibility. It is the other's choice and responsibility. Your task is to plant the seed and nurture its growth as fully as possible. But if one chooses not to continue in the way you must respect this decision and release the person while still continuing to love and care.

It is not possible for us to tell you how foolishly people scatter their forces. We see you running hither and yon throwing your vibrations to the winds. If the energy you are throwing away could be focused to bring about a harmony within, it would radiate a force field of love which would literally attract thousands. In meditation you learn to focus this power.

The inner peace you develop through meditation will shine as a beacon light onto the earth plane as well as in the higher planes. Many on the astral, and even in the higher realms, do *not know peace within themselves. If it is found on your earth plane, it is maintained throughout the other spheres.*

It is on the earth that you must learn these essential lessons of peace, brotherhood, and harmony. You must pass your tests here, either in this lifetime or another. This growth cannot be readily attained on the other planes. Even though much can be taught on the various levels between incarnations, you must then go back to the earth plane to test and try, to see whether you indeed gained the growth you were striving for.

A total peace throughout its existence on earth—this is exactly what each soul is striving for. That is why you incarnated. If you learn to become one with others and generate the peace vibration, you will have love and peace on every other plane of being. And once the earth test is finally passed, you need not return but may continue on the higher realms of existence.

The Best From Every Culture

It is time for mankind to unite. We should seek to adopt the best from every culture, every tradition, and bring them together. We must learn to think of ourselves as world citizens. It is crucial that we have universal views, to understand world religions, to know the underlying principles which unify people, not separate them.

The translations you read of any scriptures represent an individual's or several individuals' viewpoint. And you must not be bound by the period in which the scriptures may have been written. Take into consideration the time and culture of the writer. Often the writer was emphasizing dogma, or fear, to hold power over the people. The majority of the teachings are very right, however. Yet you must have ears to hear, and eyes to see.

Whether the words are found in the Bible, in the Koran, in the Bhagavad Gita, or any other sacred writings, all universal truth is the same. It is simply that God is love: you must do

119

unto others as you would have them do unto you; and love your neighbor as yourself. These are the two things which would create total peace and harmony.

Few people hear this. And yet it is in almost every language in every country, taught by every master who has ever been a channel of God.

Each of us should be able to take what is right for us from every faith, from every philosophy. We should be given the free will to take that which is suited for us at this particular time in our evolution.

We should not force our way upon anyone else. For this would only result in another form of the ritualistic, dogmatic society from which we should be trying to get away.

The churches are undergoing a tremendous transitional period at this time. What people must learn is that there is one denomination, one God, for us all. It matters not which particular master or teacher a person may be drawn to. Remember, Jesus and other masters have said, "Not me, but my Father."

It is this teaching which must be understood if universal order is to come and mankind is to live in peace. Any time there is more than one church in power, or there are various dogmatic religious beliefs, there will be wars (such as you've seen in Ireland), there will be prejudice, and a pulling apart.

God is a united One who is within all people. If we could learn to worship in the temple we carry within, then there would be no prejudice, no racial, political or religious wars. This must come if we are to survive.

The churches have badly misinterpreted the teachings in the past. The many dissections of truth have resulted in a dissected human race. We are not a whole people. This surgery of the spirit has resulted in the monstrosity of hatred. Mankind *should have* grown in the unifying spirit of love.

We still can, provided we are willing to recognize our unity from within rather than seeing differences from without.

Devastation Or Education?

Actually, we are faced with a fairly simple challenge: to devastate or to educate. By education I mean that which is universal in perspective and is based upon our caring for our fellows.

Television has had an incredible impact upon our psyches, and has done its part to accelerate the crisis which we are now facing. It can be used as a powerful tool for unification, or, as has mostly been the case, a medium for the perpetuation of violence, insensitivity and crime. People are beginning to learn that crime indeed does pay. One can get away with, at least momentarily, almost anything because of the court systems and people's indifference.

Crime represents the very opposite of what we are really supposed to be about, which is learning to use our creativity for the good. We do not have to take or desire what is someone else's. This is really not the easy way to go. The karma is much greater and heavier than we would imagine. Each one of us has the creative ability to generate whatever we want. Doing just that is learning to use our potential on the earth plane, and that is exactly what we have incarnated to do.

Our education systems have failed to develop the creative side of man, and so we feel lonely, impoverished, feeling that we cannot have what we want unless we take it from another. If this trend of crime, of ignorance in our own nature, continues, we will not have society much longer as we know it. All the policemen in the world cannot help this. It must come instead from people caring about their neighbors and working together to create the kind of life style they really want.

The process of education must eventually rest on the shoulders of the master teachers who know how to guide the individual to the university within. Although objective knowledge about the universe is now more readily obtainable, it is incidental after one has touched deeper levels of being.

Great breakthroughs are being made in the rate of learning so that a person may accumulate the necessary knowledge to

121

function in a highly specialized world. But there is the need to balance the mental man with the emotional, physical, and spiritual man. Education at its best will move into dimensional learning. All the human dimensions will be explored, understood and controlled. We must have a balanced program of growth, teaching the whole man. Then great strides will be made in re-educating people away from war, away from fear, away from hatred. We must educate our children to move toward a harmony both without and within.

The Key Is Caring

There is a sense of hopelessness today, which comes from a lack of understanding of the suffering we see around us. We find the world in confusion, and sense our inability to respond and relate to things we find offensive.

The key is for us to understand that the more light or good we give out, the more we dispel the hopelessness, meaninglessness, and negativity around us. Once we realize that the God within can and will use our channel, our life, we will literally be able to change history.

Each of us casts a light. It can spread over a mere speck of dust, or clear around the world.

Honoring the God within, or the Guru within, is what we should really be about. This has nothing to do with flaunting individuality to the exclusion of sensitivity to others. What it does mean is that we recognize that all life is part of the same Love force, and we attune to our special purpose in helping to bring about an age of peace and harmony.

As we learn to truly love the self, the eternal being within us, we are truly able to be a beacon light to others. As we follow our own inner guidance, our strength and creativity unfold. We become powerful forces for good in a world that desperately needs all the help it can get.

We have chosen to incarnate in this age because we wanted to meet the challenges that we knew would be presented to us. We wanted to make great strides in truly knowing the self, in fully accepting the responsibility and discipline necessary to achieve the greatness that is called for today. We must realize that each of us has the potential for tremendous impact upon the world, but it rests upon finding our power source within.

Each of us has free will. We may accept or reject the way to fullness of life. If we reject it, we will continue to reap disharmony, suffering, and war. We will continue to bring the results of such a choice to ourselves and others. We can choose to block a creative solution in the world crisis we all face.

But if we accept our responsibility, and ask that we be used as channels of light, we could witness a fabulous period in the history of mankind's evolution. What is *your* choice?